Railway Memories I

WEST RIDING STEAM
1955 - 1969

A pictorial diary by Robert Anderson

BELLCODE BOOKS
21 DALE AVENUE
TODMORDEN
WEST YORKSHIRE OL14 6BA

Edited by Steve Chapman

Printed by the Amadeus Press, Cleckheaton, West Yorks.

ABOVE: Class A1 No. 60156 *Great Central* in full cry storming along the centre road through Wakefield Westgate station with the 1.18pm King's Cross-Leeds at 5.1pm on 5th May, 1962.
At the time, this train rather unusually called at Wakefield Kirkgate but not Westgate, and faced a hard slog up the steep curve between the two stations. It provided a rare opportunity to hear an A1 being worked really hard as by this time East Coast main line train loadings barely tested these modern Pacifics.

Requests for photographs published in Railway Memories will be passed automatically to the copyright holder and under normal circumstances Bellcode Books itself will not reply to readers making such requests.

INTRODUCTION

Before the 1974 local government reorganisation, the West Riding of Yorkshire was a vast county embracing the cities of Leeds, Sheffield, Bradford, Wakefield and Ripon plus numerous large towns.

In railway terms it reached all the way from just south of Sheffield to half way up the Settle and Carlisle line, to Ripon in the north, to the port of Goole in the east, and in the west to the Pennine cotton town of Todmorden and even to the very edge of Oldham.

Its industrial wealth and strategic position on crossroads between north-south and east-west routes led to it being served by a host of railway companies - the Midland, the Great Northern, the North Eastern, the Great Central, the London & North Western, the Lancashire & Yorkshire, the Hull & Barnsley and the Great Eastern plus several joint lines which these various companies operated between them. With them came a great diversity of steam locomotives and operations which lasted into the 1960s.

In **Railway Memories No.16** Robert Anderson takes us on a chronological journey through the pain and the glory of the last 15 years of British Railways steam operation in the West Riding.

These were years when the pain of decline was tempered by the glory of steam locomotives being called on to stand in for ailing and frequently nigh-useless diesels, when Bradford was served by some of Britain's very last steam-hauled London trains, and when the last of Stanier's celebrated Jubilees continued to power long-distance expresses over steeply graded West Riding lines as late as the summer of 1967.

"No other machine in its day has been a more faithful friend to mankind nor has contributed more to the growth of industry." Mr. R. F. Hanks, chairman of the British Transport Commission Western Area Board, speaking at Swindon Works on 18th March, 1960 during the naming of *Evening Star*, the last steam locomotive built for British Railways.

Note: BR used the 24-hour clock in its working timetables from 7. 9. 1964 so in Railway Memories we do the same.

All photographs in this latest Railway Memories book were taken by Robert Anderson between 1955 and 1969. This is him, looking very businesslike, with Ivatt Class 4 2-6-0 No. 43044 at Bradford Manningham shed on 28th April, 1967, the day before the depot's complete closure.

DRAMA & DECLINE

THE former West Riding of Yorkshire's industrial wealth attracted all the major northern railway companies and each one brought its own highly individual locomotives.

Through the pages of Trains Illustrated I realised that it was these very locomotives of the old pre-1923 grouping companies which were being withdrawn from service, and it was these that caught my imagination. Not for me the sleek streamlined A4s or the handsome Royal Scots. My pocket money was juggled between film and train tickets to photograph or ride behind woebegone Midland Compounds or the hardy Ivatt GNR N1 0-6-2 tanks. To me, the N1s with their harsh staccato bark were the epitome of the Great Northern Railway - and a source of much intrigue as to why such 40-odd year-old engines should work Bradford-King's Cross expresses over the severely graded Dewsbury route whilst almost new and more powerful B1 4-6-0s worked similar trains taking the easier route via Morley Top. Sadly, the N1s had all gone by early 1959 and it was left to the J6 goods engines and the J50 and J52 tanks to keep the GN flag flying in the West Riding.

My affection for the Compounds began with a chance photograph taken at Bradford's Manningham engine sheds in January, 1955. My parents had just bought me a Kodak Duaflex camera, a sort of basic reflex camera which took 2 1/4 inch square negatives. Optically, it wasn't even as good as the much joked about Brownie 127 but it was better than nothing.

I had just "snapped" Class 5 4-6-0 No. 44900, visiting from Carlisle Kingmoor, when a head popped out and asked if there was any chance of a print. I duly obliged and this was the beginning of a lifetime's friendship with passed fireman Ivan Maltby who gradually introduced me to the wonderful world of footplating.

First it was just "cabbing" at Manningham shed or Bradford Forster Square station but even this included Jubilees and once a Royal Scot on a filling-in turn. I was still only 10 when I had my first cab ride, with Fairburn 2-6-4 tank 42051 running light engine from Manningham to Bradford. This soon gravitated to Bradford-Skipton runs but best of all was the odd run on one of my beloved Compounds. They weren't really the genuine article for the last Midland Railway Compound was withdrawn in 1953 but following its formation in 1923, the London Midland & Scottish Railway was so impressed by the performance of these engines that it built 195 of its own and it was these that were finishing off their days on the Morecambe-Leeds/Bradford service.

I photographed 41113 minus her front driving wheels on Leeds Holbeck shed in July, 1958. She was in absolutely dreadful condition and I later learned that she had just been transferred to Lancaster from Rugby, no doubt having been in store. Eight days later, on 27th July, I was at the end of platform 5/6 of Leeds City Wellington station(that well known spotters' pitch) when my eyes popped out of my head. Backing down to work an excursion from Northampton forward to Bradford was this rusting hulk, and sure enough it was 41113. I jumped aboard the train, private excursion or not, and was treated to a 16 1/4 minute dash to Shipley with ten coaches behind the tender. After turning at Forster Square in just 48 minutes she headed back to Leeds with the 3.52pm St. Pancras express and excelled again by doing Shipley to Leeds in a shade over 15 minutes - and with nine mark 1 coaches in tow. Talk about life in the old dog and for that matter sheer professionalism and dedication by driver and fireman in coaxing such a performance out of an apparent wreck. No. 41113 was withdrawn from service four months later and the very last Compound working in regular service was Sheffield Millhouses 40907 which was steamed for the 9.5am Sheffield to Derby on Sunday, 21st August, 1960. On 16th September she made one final journey under her own power to Doncaster for scrap. The Midland remained well represented though, by a surprisingly large fleet of vintage 0-6-0s.

Another of the all-time classic British steam locomotive types about to fade into history so far as the West Riding was concerned, was the Radial 2-4-2T of the old Lancashire & Yorkshire Railway. These locos were not only numerically the largest but also the most successful of this wheel arrangement ever to grace our railways. Their feats of haulage with heavy and tightly timed commuter trains operated by that company are legendary and the curator of historical relics at the British Transport Commission saw fit to order one for official preservation as part of the National Collection. Now at the National Railway Museum in York and highly polished as L&Y No. 1008, it was in fact once Manningham engine No. 50621 which worked trains to Leeds, Ilkley, Skipton and Barnoldswick.

Towards the end of 1956 several were still active from Manningham, Low Moor, Sowerby Bridge and Huddersfield, and probably their last *regular* job was for one of the Sowerby Bridge locos on the 12 noon from Bradford Exchange.

During 1957 their appearances became spasmodic, the Huddersfield locos appearing the most with trips to Wakefield and Normanton. At times of acute motive power shortage they were pressed into express

Where it all began. Robert Anderson was just 10 years old when he took this shot of D49/2 4-4-0 No. 62742 *The Braes of Derwent* preparing to leave Leeds Central with the down Harrogate Sunday Pullman at 1.20pm on 30th January, 1955. The photo won a prize in a competition organised by the long defunct Yorkshire Observer Budget newspaper, and was his first published picture.

passenger duty - on the 7.15pm Wakefield Westgate to Huddersfield, a connection with the down West Riding from King's Cross.

The last two active members, 50725 and 50865, went into store in April, 1958 with seven out of the eight remaining Yorkshire-based locos being withdrawn in October. All seven made a melancholy journey to Crewe Works for scrapping but the works couldn't cope and they were dumped in the old goods yard sidings at Badnall Wharf near Stafford. They languished here for eight months before being sold on to a private breaker - A. Loom (Ellis Metals Ltd.) at Spondon, near Derby.

As a young spotter I turned my nose up at York. Everyone went there and I thought it was common. Doncaster was much better class and if one made the effort to catch one of the early trains from Bradford, there was a good chance of a very fast run from Wakefield behind an A1 Pacific.

On arrival at Donny, it was hot foot to the south end bay platforms for one of the main events of the day -

the 9.7am departure for Spalding which produced a Sandringham 4-6-0. These Gresley 1928 designed locos were highly sought after for by then they were exclusive to the Great Eastern lines. Those allocated to March depot, however, found their way further north and were a daily sight at Sheffield Victoria with the Harwich to Liverpool boat train. There they handed over to electric locos for the journey over the Woodhead line to Manchester. These two workings provided the only regular sightings of the Sandringhams in the West Riding but ceased in 1959 when the locos became one of the first major London & North Eastern Railway classes to fall victim to modernisation.

By way of the GN & GE Joint line via Lincoln, the Great Eastern Railway made its way to Doncaster where it once leased quite a large engine shed. This presence was revived in the late 1950s when Doncaster received a temporary allocation of Great Eastern shunting engines.

The old West Riding was one of the first parts of

A highlight of any visit to Doncaster in the 1950s was the sight of a Class B17 Sandringham 4-6-0 on the 9.7am stopping train to Spalding. Here, at 8.27am on 21st February, 1959 B17/6 No. 61620 *Clumber,* **one of those rebuilt from the 1928 originals with B1 boilers from 1947 onwards, waits to get the train on its way .** *Clumber* **was withdrawn less than seven months later and was scrapped at Stratford Works in London.**

British Railways to receive diesel and electric traction yet, interestingly, it became one of the last to dispense with steam for in 1960 veteran steam locos from no less than seven pre-grouping companies were still at work in the county. No other area outside London could boast this at such a late stage in the history of the British steam locomotive.

Fleet modernisation started in early 1952 when the purpose-built depot at Wath opened its doors to the new electric Bo-Bos(later to become Class 76) for the Manchester-Sheffield-Wath electrification, officially dubbed Britain's first all electric main line.

Further history was made in 1954 when the first of BR's lightweight diesel railcars were allocated to Bradford's Bowling depot, commencing a half-hourly interval service between Bradford Exchange and Leeds Central on 14th June.

In January, 1955 the BTC announced its £1,200 million Modernisation Plan. This was to be the saviour of Britain's railways and was intended to combat the private motor car, the aeroplane with package holidays to near guaranteed sunshine and, probably most of all, the heavy lorry. So far as motive power was concerned, the intention was for a pilot scheme whereby 170-odd main line diesel locomotives of three different power groups supplied by various manufacturers were to be thoroughly tried and tested in service over a period of three years with the most successful being mass produced, culminating in 2,500 main line diesels by 1970. This was an excellent plan - if only it had been implemented.

The Plan envisaged the progressive replacement of steam locomotives by electric and diesel traction over 15 years but it estimated that around 7,000 steam locomotives would still be in service by 1970. Less than a year after the Plan had been presented it became apparent that it was not going to stem the flood of traffic towards the roads or the airlines and it was reappraised in 1956, and again in 1959. The government placed the railways in the strange and unenviable position whereby they were expected to be both a public service and a commercial undertaking, making it clear that financial support was not unlimited. The most important single feature of the Plan, the sensible progressive replacement of steam, was abandoned. The three year trial period for the new diesel locomotives was dropped and their introduction was accelerated to the fastest pace at which the manufacturers could supply them, a pace which outstripped the BR regions' ability to maintain them properly.

The first of the original pilot scheme main line diesels into the West Riding arrived in 1958 - the English Electric Type 4s. Weighing 133 tons and 67ft long, they were impressive looking machines, but it immediately became apparent that their performance out on the road was not nearly so impressive.

Nevertheless, more and more were ordered, the BTC believing that salvation from BR's declining financial fortunes lay in getting rid of steam as rapidly as possible. From the start of the winter 1958 timetable in September, the EE4s were put on to five cyclic diagrams demanding 4,500 miles a week from each locomotive. They couldn't do it and the intensive diagrams had to be dropped.

More and more untried diesels arrived, probably the most disastrous being the Crossley - engined Metropolitan Vickers Co-Bos D5700 - 19 which eventually began regular service in March, 1959 double-heading the overnight Hendon-Gushetfaulds Condor express freight. Each night, the Up and Down trains were due to pass near Shipley at around half-past

midnight so few people saw them, except when a failure resulted in one of the Metrovicks lurking in a siding somewhere awaiting a tow back to Derby. By the middle of 1960 nearly a third of the class was stored unserviceable pending an agreement between BR and the builders over the maintenance and repair of these unfortunate locomotives. Indeed, the last one to be built, D5719, was just six months old when it was placed in store.

That year dawned with more and more EE4s lumbering about, most local passenger services in the hands of diesel railcars, or DMUs as they were becoming known, while diesel shunters were increasingly taking over yard and pilot duties. Yet a surprising number of elderly steam locomotives still clung to life. Most freight and express passenger trains were still steam hauled, the last new steam locomotive had only just been built and the main line diesel fleet continued to disappoint, both in terms of its performance and its availability. Nowhere was this more apparent than on the East Coast main line which passed through Doncaster and Selby on its way between King's Cross, Newcastle and Edinburgh. The rejuvinated but by now quite elderly Gresley

The abysmal performance of BR's new diesels contributed greatly to the West Riding steam scene of the 1950s and 1960s. Among the worst offenders were the Metrovick Co-Bos which worked the overnight Condor express container train through the county on its way between London and Glasgow. Failure of one of these locomotives would present local enthusiasts with the rare chance of a daytime photo, such as this shot of a disgraced D5710 languishing in Bradford's Manningham shed yard at 5.30pm on 7th August, 1959, after failing at Bingley the previous night.

Pacifics together with the more modern Peppercorn A1s were proving quite the equal of the EE4s on the famous racing grounds. It must have been a great embarrassment for the authorities that the route's most prestigious train, The Elizabethan - the world's longest daily non-stop run - had to remain steam hauled.

People were beginning to wonder if the end of steam really was nigh but 1961 was to prove conclusively that it was. From 2nd January a new Hull-Leeds-Liverpool service was introduced operated by high-powered Inter-City type DMUs known as the Trans-Pennines which afforded a high level of comfort and, for the time, quite phenomenal acceleration. On the same day, the entire Newcastle-Liverpool service was handed over to EE4s and in one stroke the number of timetabled steam passenger trains calling at busy Huddersfield had been cut to 14 a day.

At the same time, a new beast came on the scene in the form of the Peak class diesel electric and here at last was a diesel which could thrash the living day-lights out of the best of British steam. Originally based at Leeds Neville Hill depot pending the installation of maintenance facilities at Holbeck, they began working Leeds-St. Pancras services in accordance with the Midland Lines dieselisation programme. Then came the Deltics and with their arrival the ECML completed a hat trick. It already had the world's fastest steam locomotive - the A4 *Mallard* - and the world's longest non-stop daily passenger train, now it also had the world's most powerful single unit diesel electric locomotive.

1961 was to see the swansong of steam on the ECML although it did continue to play an important part on the Leeds-King's Cross expresses until June, 1963. What a year steam had. One was bound to wonder if someone somewhere was trying to rock the boat just a little bit for the steam locos positively glistened with the majority of principal named trains seeing regular steam haulage. Once again, the Elizabethan was steam-hauled and there was but one failure en-route during the entire service. If only the new diesels were so reliable.

This continued unreliability was undoubtably the cause for the laugh of the year. The Duke and Duchess of Kent's wedding at York Minster on 8th June saw the Royal Train from King's Cross headed by A4 60028 *Walter K. Wigham* and two other trains conveying special guests by 60003 *Andrew K. McCosh* and 60015 *Quicksilver*. The condition the locomotives were turned out in, even by Royal Train standards, simply beggared belief. Even the cab roofs and tender sheetings were painted white. To rub further salt in the wound, rumours were rife that all preceeding diesel-hauled trains had fitters aboard!

It was to be June, 1963 before steam finally bade

farewell to the ECML and it was fitting that the important section to Wakefield, Leeds and Bradford had the honour of seeing the last steam-hauled expresses from King's Cross.

The Midland main line was less glamorous than the ECML but it traversed the West Riding for 106 miles from entering south of Sheffield, at Dore, to leaving just north of Garsdale on the Settle and Carlisle.

It only had one class of Type 4 diesel allocated to it - the 2,500hp Peaks. The first arrived in Leeds during the last days of 1960 and over the next 18 months, Midland Lines depots took delivery at the rate of nearly two per week. Staff simply could not be trained at this rate and the farcical state of affairs arose where depots were crammed full of idle diesels awaiting exam or repair while steam locomotives had to be pressed into service on express passenger trains. I well remember a visit to Holbeck shed in March, 1962. The yard was packed with idle Peaks as a green jacketed diesel driver prepared a Crewe North Royal Scot to work the Up Thames-Clyde Express south from Leeds. The headboard was lying against the coaler and I asked him: "Aren't you going to put the headboard on?"

He replied: "Nay lad, I can't be bothered. Just look around you."

Matters were made even worse, for as he spoke a Peak trundled past with a two-coach Cudworth to Leeds stopping train.

The third principal main line to traverse the West Riding was the much lamented Great Central which passed through Penistone and Sheffield Victoria on its way from Manchester to London Marylebone which it reached as recently as 1899. Its closure by stealth started in 1960 and six years later there were no through services using the line. Virtually trouble-free electric locomotives had taken over the Sheffield-Manchester passenger service through a newly-built Woodhead tunnel from 20th September, 1954 but the Sheffield-Nottingham section continued to provide work for steam. In the late 1950s, even in 1960, it still saw not only the handsome ex-GC Director 4-4-0s but also some of the last remaining ex-GNR K2 2-6-0s.

The Directors have been described as one of this country's most outstanding 4-4-0s and it is fitting that the one chosen for official preservation in the National Collection, 62660 *Butler Henderson*, ended its days working off Sheffield Darnall shed.

The GC was renowned for the quality build of its locomotives and this shows in the longevity of its J11 0-6-0s - nicknamed "Pom Poms" - some being 60 years old when withdrawn, not to mention its original Robinson Class O4 2-8-0s, some of which outlived the very locomotives that were meant to replace them. This is no reflection on the BR Standard 9F

The prestigous Elizabethan which ran the 392.9 miles between King's Cross and Edinburgh non-stop remained steam-hauled until the end of the 1961 summer timetable, partly because the Type 4 diesels were not up to it but also because only the A4 Pacifics with their corridor tenders allowed the crews to change without the train having to stop. The Deltics were too noisy for the relief crew to ride in the rear cab. Here, well-groomed 60032 *Gannet* runs proudly through Selby ahead of time with the southbound run at 1.22pm on 22nd July, 1960.

2-10-0s but a reflection on the sad state of affairs that had led to steam locomotives with a useful life expectancy of 40 years being withdrawn after just six and a half years.

No express passenger locos from the Lancashire & Yorkshire and London & North Western railways remained by the mid-1950s and, indeed, there were no LNW locomotives allocated to the West Riding. However, its famous Super D 0-8-0 goods engines were still trudging across the Pennines from the Manchester, Stockport and, surprisingly the Carnforth, directions until early 1962.

Besides the Radials, a number of smaller L&Y tank engines were still at work, most notably the diminutive 0-4-0 saddletanks - the "Pugs" - at Goole Docks, but it was Aspinall's 0-6-0 tender engines from a design dating back to 1889 which lasted the longest in the West Riding - until the end of 1962 in fact.

Following the closure of Selby and Starbeck sheds in 1959, the North Eastern Railway was represented by just one depot in the West Riding - Leeds Neville Hill. The graceful D20 4-4-0s were gone by 1957 followed by the lovely little G5 0-4-4Ts the next year. All that remained were the magnificent original

Raven B16 4-6-0s, the hard working Q6 0-8-0 mineral engines and a handful of J71 and J72 0-6-0Ts at the ex-Midland Normanton shed. Q6s 63420 and 63426 were the last pre-grouping locomotives allocated to and still working in the West Riding before being transferred to Tyne Dock for further use in October, 1966.

The years 1962 to the end in 1968 were naturally sad but nonetheless interesting. A few vintage steam locos still rubbed shoulders with more modern steam and diesel traction while in 1962 the Deltic-hauled West Riding was still often banked out of Leeds Central by a GN J6 about 45 years the Deltic's elder.

The absolutely appalling availability of the Peaks continued unabated and resulted in some most interesting steam substitutes: LNER Pacifics and V2 2-6-2s at Birmingham New Street and Royal Scots at Newcastle on North East-South West expresses. A V2 even occasionally visited St. Pancras. With Jubilees deputising on the Midland main line, some days at Sheffield Midland produced a continuous procession of steam hauled expresses, most of which should have been diesel hauled.

It was the same on Liverpool - Newcastle services

Classic North Eastern in the West Riding. An original Raven B16/1 4-6-0, No. 61428, storms past Osmondthorpe on the outskirts of Leeds with a packed 13-coach excursion to the east coast at 11.33am on 6th June, 1960. The variety of rolling stock was typical of such extra summer trains which were frequently formed of coaches kept in store throughout the winter.
Although predominantly based at York, B16s were also allocated at various times to at least four West Riding sheds - Neville Hill, Mirfield, Selby and Starbeck.

with Jubilee and Class 5 4-6-0s sometimes working throughout. The Geordies couldn't reciprocate so easily due to the restricted route availability(RA9) of their Pacifics and V2s but an A3 did once make it to Manchester Exchange although the platform coping stones at Miles Platting station suffered in the process. At the subsequent inquiry the deputy chief controller was heard to mutter: "RA9? What the bloody hell does RA9 mean?."

In the winter, considerable trouble was experienced with the Spanner train heating boilers on the Peaks which resulted in some spectacular steam-diesel double heading over the Trans-Pennine route when a steam loco was attached, usually behind the diesel, to provide train heating. If the steam locomotive and, more importantly, its crew were up to it there could be some remarkable running. I have some wonderful memories of dark, cold nights at Diggle as the 17.05 Liverpool-Newcastle express stormed up the long bank through Saddleworth hooting and whistling for

the boarded crossing there. You could see the great column of smoke and steam before the train came into view, then the loco headlamps and the lights of the carriages as they stormed round the curve alongside the canal. It then swept past the signal box with the signalman doubtless wishing all trains would clear his section so quickly, and the Class 5's fireman, having just put his shovel down for they were nearly at the summit, glancing enviously at the nearby Diggle Hotel which would be in full swing.

Another source of entertainment was the arrival of classes previously rare in the West Riding. A trio of the rather ungainly Thompson L1 2-6-4Ts displaced by diesels in the south had been re-allocated to Doncaster by 1960 and in 1961 further examples from the North East were a Christmas present to Low Moor and Ardsley sheds. Intended to replace the ageing J50s, they were both unsuitable and unpopular. Their long wheelbase caused numerous derailments in the yards so instead they added variety to

10

the motive power on the Bradford portions of King's Cross trains.

New diesel facilities had opened at Sheffield Darnall and by the summer of 1962, 90 main line diesel locomotives and almost as many diesel shunters were allocated there. By the year end the Brush Type 4s(now Class 47s) had entered service and it wasn't long before these too were at Darnall.

With dieselisation on this scale it was of course inevitable that there would be massive withdrawals of steam locomotives. Commonsense had initially prevailed for the first to go were the remaining pre-Grouping classes which were in any case worn out and redundant through line closures and declining traffic as much as dieselisation and electrification. The Gresley D49 4-4-0s were one early victim among later types but their complicated valve gear must have been expensive to maintain and that alone would have been a good reason for their demise. The withdrawal programme for the A3 Pacifics was suspended and many earmarked for scrapping were put through works to help out the ailing Type 4 diesels. Similarly, on the London Midland Region, the decision to withdraw some 7P 4-6-0s was reversed. Nonetheless, between 1960 and 1962 almost 5,700 steam locomotives were withdrawn.

One cannot help but wonder if this was an account-ancy procedure with the regions being told to drastically reduce their steam stock to prepare for the new regime of the British Railways Board which came into being on 1st January, 1963. For in the last six months of 1962 over TWO THOUSAND steam locomotives were withdrawn including no less than 57 B1s in October alone.

These moves may well have pleased the politicians and accountants but many experienced railway operators and mechanical engineers were expressing disquiet. Figures released by the BTC before its demise showed a disturbing 16.2 per cent of diesel electric locomotives out of action awaiting attention while the corresponding figures for the allegedly outdated and inefficient steam fleet was little worse at 19.8 per cent.

The appalling weather of early 1963 saw the availability of, for example, the Midland Lines Peaks, drop to below 50 per cent with Jubilees in dreadful condition being dragged out of store to take their place. Some DMU services were steam worked, even by goods engines and the whole dieselisation policy seemed to lay in tatters. Never had so much been held together by so little. Morale was low, for much of the remaining steam fleet was in a terrible state and was becoming despised by many through no fault of its own.

New English Electric Type 4 diesels turned out to be a disappointment on the East Coast main line and so the route's famous Pacifics enjoyed an extended spell of glory, putting up the sort of daily performances that BR had expected of the diesels.
A3 No. 60039 *Sandwich* **is seen approaching Wakefield Westgate with the 12.55pm Leeds to King's Cross on 2nd March, 1963 during her final days of service. She was one of those engines which excelled, maintaining the Type 4 diesel diagrams, completing 100,000 miles between works visits and finally clocking up over 1.5 million miles by the time she was withdrawn.**

Matters were little better by early 1965 and the BRB was reluctantly obliged to put a number of class 5 and 6 steam locos through works in order to fulfil its summer timetable. As an economy measure some were turned out unlined and unvarnished and looked pretty drab - but at least they were clean for a few weeks and leaked steam only from the safety valves.

By 1966 whole areas, indeed Regions, were totally devoid of steam traction but the West Riding still had much of interest to offer. For a short time in January, 1966, the Post Office-controlled 21.50 York to Aberystwyth and Liverpool mail train was officially diagrammed to be double headed from Leeds to Stalybridge by a Farnley Junction steam locomotive and a Holbeck Peak. This must have been a pretty unique diagram but it didn't last long for by early February the train was in the hands of a Peak assisted by an English Electric Type 4.

Low Moor shed was getting a reputation for clean engines - a rarity indeed. Just who actually cleaned them is a matter for conjecture as there were rumours of highly organised cleaning gangs descending on depots. Blackpool seemed a centre for such activity for in the morning filthy engines could work an excursion to the resort from the Leeds, Bradford or Wakefield area and return in the evening positively gleaming. Sometimes they were cleaned on one side only - always the side facing the sun.

Dismay and glee were the contrasting reactions when it became obvious that steam would again be required to work some of this year's summer Saturday passenger trains, but it came as no surprise for those in the know. For example, on Friday 1st July, 1966 just 13 of the 25 Peaks allocated to Holbeck were available for traffic. This indicates that these locomotives were still experiencing teething problems in their fifth year of service!

We had quite a choice of steam workings over a variety of routes. Probably the most popular was the Saturdays Only Poole-Bradford which was Jubilee-hauled from Nottingham to Bradford Exchange. The first coach resembled a recording studio with microphones and heads adorned with knotted handkerchiefs being thrust out of just about every window. The show got off with a good thrash up the Midland main line to Bradway Tunnel but the main event was the fearful restart from Barnsley up to Summer Lane. This was on a tree-lined curving bank as steep as 1 in 41 and on at least one damp day the large wheeled Jubilee got bogged down. More was to come with the 1 in 45/50 from Greetland up to Dryclough Junction although an assisting engine was provided for this section. Leaving Halifax, some very fast running often resulted in Bradford being reached in 14

Steam/diesel combinations were a regular feature of expresses on the Trans-Pennine route with troublesome diesels frequently needing help from the steam locos they were supposed to have replaced.
At 10.53 on 28th May, 1965 BR Standard Class 5 4-6-0 No. 73163 was vigorously assisting Peak Type 4 No. D190 away from Huddersfield with the 09.00 Liverpool-Newcastle. The steam loco, from Manchester's Patricroft shed and probably co-opted from duty as Manchester Exchange station pilot, was fulfilling the dual role of heating the train and assisting the ailing diesel.

Looking at this picture it is hard to believe that the total end of BR steam was only 12 months away. At 11am on 5th August, 1967, celebrity Jubilee No. 45562 *Alberta*, in utterly immaculate condition, roars along the Leeds-Shipley line past Swaine Woods, Calverley, with the Saturdays Only 06.40 Birmingham-Glasgow. That summer, one of Holbeck's surviving Jubilees regularly worked this train between Leeds and Carlisle.

minutes with seven coaches behind the tender. Today's modern two-car diesel units are booked to do this section just one minute quicker.

Another train very popular with travellers and photographers alike was the Saturdays Only 06.40 Birmingham-Glasgow which was a Holbeck Jubilee from Leeds to Glasgow. Again, the running could be of a very high order with up to 25 minutes being gained on the schedule. Enthusiasts travelled overnight from the far ends of the country to ride in the leading coach. Unfortunately, the level of fare evasion was very high - until someone had a word in the right lughole. I have never seen a travelling ticket inspector do so much business for by Blea Moor he was still only half way down the train.

By now the West Riding had become one of the best places in Britain to see and hear steam locomotives hard at work but the last day of the summer timetable, Saturday 3rd September, 1966, was a sombre occasion for everyone. The Poole-Bradford had gone out in fine style with the celebrity *Alberta* gaining 13 minutes from Nottingham with the driver sounding suitable whistle salvos on leaving both Huddersfield and Halifax - and many did wonder if this was more or less the end of the steam-hauled express passenger train in the West Riding.

November 5th saw the last run of the afternoon Bradford-Stockport and its return evening working. Over the years this train - especially its evening return from Stockport - had gained a reputation for some very lively running with its Low Moor men and their competent Fairburn 2-6-4Ts. Its withdrawal was a blow to the timing fraternity.

It was by now obvious that the West Riding was going to be one of the last parts of BR with steam. This was due in no small measure to it being served by three different regions, the London Midland, Eastern and North Eastern, but on 1st January, 1967 the Eastern and North Eastern regions merged with the latter losing its identity. The Eastern Region was already well advanced with the elimination of steam and things didn't look as rosy as at this time last year.

Christmas 1966, the New Year 1967 and the Easter holidays came and went with most of the holiday reliefs booked to steam but actually diesel worked. Had diesel availability finally got its act together?

There did however continue to be quite a lot of steam activity, mainly around Leeds and Bradford on passenger trains, and over the Diggle and Calder Valley routes with freights to and from Healey Mills marshalling yard.

In July, 1967 the Bradford portion of the Yorkshire Pullman became Britain's last steam-hauled Pullman train. Low Moor Class 5 4-6-0 No. 45208 was making easy work of the 1 in 50 climb out of Bradford Exchange with the five-coach train at 09.57 on 30th May, 1967.

The locomotives were in appalling condition and it is a tribute to the very nature of the steam locomotive that they were able to carry out their duties. Despite this, there were still occasional magnificent runs. On 31st March, 1967 I was lucky enough to be on the 09.00 Bradford Exchange to King's Cross express which was to be worked to Leeds Central by Fairburn tank No. 42233, known as the "Crackpot engine" because of its deplorable condition. The load was only three coaches but it was a nasty damp rail and despite some slipping up the 1 in 49 to St. Dunstans, Hammerton Street driver Frank Bastow - better known for his rendition of Ilkley Moor B'at'At on the horns of a DMU - succeeded in half killing his fireman and passing Laisterdyke station in 5 1/4 minutes from a cold start right at the very end of Bradford Exchange's platform 5.

The closure of Manningham shed on 29th April, 1967 and the transfer of all through services away from Bradford Forster Square to Exchange was a major blow. This was all part of the Leeds City combination scheme which also involved the complete closure of Leeds Central on 1st May, 1967.

One interesting by-product of this was the 07.45 from King's Cross which continued as the complete train to Bradford, producing another official steam/diesel combination in the form of a 2-6-4T and

a Sulzer Type 2. I recall discussing this with a very pro-diesel traction inspector who reluctantly admitted they(the diesel crew) needed the "mobile kettle" to get them up the bank through Holbeck to Armley.

Whitsuntide produced a whole string of Class 5s on excursion traffic but best of all, Jubilee *Alberta* was used for Royal Train duties on Tuesday 30th May to convey the Duke of Edinburgh to Nidd Bridge, north of Harrogate. This rather surprising feat was due largely to the efforts of the enthusiastic traction engineer at Leeds, Tom Greaves, who had a knack of convincing his seniors to do things his way. This was no doubt why three of Holbeck's Jubilees were kept in suitable condition to again work the summer Saturday reliefs over the Settle & Carlisle.

On 10th July, the full electric service started on the Southern Region's main line from Waterloo to Bournemouth and the magnificent reign of the Bulleid Pacifics was over. From this day on, the West Riding offered the richest selection of steam-hauled passenger trains anywhere in the country. The 1 in 49/50 start out of Bradford Exchange became a favourite with photographers for on a Saturday morning there were up to 11 steam-hauled departures in the space of two and a half hours. Some were diagrammed to diesel traction but were more often than not steam. The highlight was the simultaneous departure at 08.20 of trains to both Skegness and Bridlington. A whip-round usually ensured the driver of the lighter loaded Skegness train held back to ensure a neck and neck climb past the ensemble at Mill Lane. The icing on the cake was that there was still time to photograph the immaculate Jubilee roaring along the nearby Aire Valley with the 06.40 Birmingham-Glasgow. Add to this 11 daytime Saturday Only trains over Diggle plus the Halifax-King's Cross and its return working and it is easy to see why the West Riding suddenly became so popular. All these trains involved uphill slogging so it was a tape recorder's paradise too.

It was all to come to a very quick end. The summer timetable finished on 3rd September and one month later, Sunday 1st October was to be the last day of steam operation on public passenger services in the West Riding. Holbeck, Normanton and Low Moor all lost their steam allocations, the latter closing completely. To cater for steam engines working into the area from the London Midland Region - now the last BR region with a steam allocation - limited servicing facilities were retained at Normanton until the end of the year.

Alberta then had another Royal Train job. She left Holbeck light engine on 18th October, 1967 for Newcastle but en-route she was commandeered to assist a diesel which had failed with a freight train near Darlington.

The nails were being banged into the coffin at the rate of one a month now for Saturday 4th November saw the last steam engine on the last day of steam operation at the last steam depot, not only in the West Riding but on the Eastern Region. Royston's 8F 2-8-0 No. 48276, a long time West Riding resident, worked the 15.00 Carlton-Goole freight, returned home in the darkness light engine and dropped her fire for the last time.

There were still some steam-hauled freights working in from the LMR, from Heysham and across the Pennines both on the Diggle and Calder Valley routes, while the Standard Class 4 4-6-0s were still active on the Grassington branch.

The few remaining steam passenger turns received a tremedous boost over the Christmas holiday for all the reliefs between the North East and Manchester, for which the LMR provided the power over the Pennines, were diagrammed to steam. There were

By summer 1968 cross-Pennine freight trains via the Calder Valley were among the very last steam workings on British Rail, using locomotives from the surviving Lancashire steam sheds, such as Rose Grove at Burnley. At 11.40 on 3rd December, 1966, WD 2-8-0 No. 90233 pulls its heavy coal train round the sharp curve from Hall Royd Junction to Stansfield Hall, Todmorden, to await the assistance of a banking engine for the gruelling 1 in 65 slog up to Copy Pit summit and Lancashire.

three on Saturday 23rd December and four on Boxing Day, all shown as Class 5s.

I duly made a sentimental journey to Leeds City on Boxing Day to witness what I had decided might well be the last steam-hauled long distance public express passenger train to run in Yorkshire, let alone the West Riding. The previous relief, 1M72 15.28 Newcastle to Manchester had left Leeds behind a Carlisle Kingmoor Britannia instead of the diagrammed Class 5 so of course everybody piled aboard that, leaving the platform clear for me to set up my tripod and photograph Newton Heath's 45255 waiting to work forward with 1M74, the 17.22 Darlington-Manchester relief. The driver popped his head out and asked if there was any chance of a print. Quick as a flash I answered back: "Any chance of a ride?"

Driver Walter Scarth seemed happy with this deal. I thought I'd got the better part of it but never mind. We left Leeds to a tremendous salvo of farewell hoots from all the diesels and I soon realised the awful condition this engine was in. The knock was so bad that the whole cab lurched from side to side with each revolution. How the fireman kept his balance I just don't know but he never missed the firebox door once. I was glad to sit down and hang on! As we rattled our way down through Batley I was mesmerised by the approaching shower of sparks and steam and the two little dots of light on the front buffer beam of 73000 as it stormed past us with 1N67, the 17.40 Manchester-Newcastle relief - the penultimate diagrammed steam public express passenger train into Leeds.

1968 dawned and the LMR still sent steam over with freight via Diggle, the Calder Valley and from Heysham but there were problems as Normanton shed had closed for good on New Year's Eve and there was nowhere for them to be serviced.

It was a year of bulled up locomotives and railtours as everybody paid their own farewells culminating in the now famous "15 Guinea Special" of 11th August from Liverpool to Carlisle and back, with 70013 *Oliver Cromwell* outward and Class 5s 44871 and 44781 for the return. And that was it, apart from the now famous exploits of *Flying Scotsman* which for the next four years was the only privately-owned steam locomotive allowed to run on BR lines.

With driver Scarth on the footplate, desperately run-down Class 5 No. 45255 waits at Leeds City to take over the 17.22 Darlington-Manchester relief on Boxing Day, 1967. This was probably the last steam-hauled long-distance public passenger train to leave Leeds.

ABOVE: 13TH JUNE, 1955. The year 1955 saw the 17-day strike by engine crews called by the Association of Locomotive Engineers & Firemen. Very few trains ran and the sheer numbers of idle locomotives outstripped the ability of depots to accommodate them so they were lined up in various sidings around the network giving enthusiasts the chance to witness large gatherings in some unusual places.
With the loco yard at Bradford Manningham full to capacity these classic engines were placed in the nearby Manningham sidings. From the front are: Stanier Class 3 2-6-2T No. 40162, Johnson Midland 2P 4-4-0 No. 40552(originally built at Derby in 1901 but later rebuilt,) LMS Compound 4-4-0 No. 41196, LMS 4F 0-6-0 No. 44431, Compounds 41137 and 41063, Midland 3F 0-6-0s 43686 and 43784, Stanier Class 3 2-6-2Ts 4011 4 and 40178, Midland 4F 0-6-0 No. 43906, and LMS 4Fs 44181 and 44207.

BELOW: 5TH APRIL, 1956, 3.23PM. Class 8P Coronation Pacific No. 46225 *Duchess of Gloucester* took part in trials on the Settle & Carlisle line. Not only was it the first visit of that class to the route but the trials, involving two firemen and equivalent loads behind the tender of 900 tons, provided the greatest continuous effort ever produced by a British steam locomotive.
With tender sheeted over, 46225 is pictured passing through Bingley with the mobile test units in tow after turning on Shipley triangle because she was too long for Skipton's 60ft turntable.

LEFT: 27TH OCTOBER, 1956, 11.30AM. By 1956 the last regular working for a Lancashire & Yorkshire 2-4-2T was the 12 noon Bradford Exchange to Sowerby Bridge stopping train. No. 50752 from 25E Sowerby Bridge shed, has just taken water before coupling up to the train.

BELOW: 1ST JUNE, 1957. Another classic at Bradford Exchange. Ex-Great Northern N1 0-6-2T No. 69472, from Ardsley shed, begins its journey on the 10.50am to King's Cross which it will work as far as Wakefield Westgate via Batley and Dewsbury. On the left, a 'Black Five' 4-6-0 simmers with the 11.15 to Liverpool which will combine with the 10.55 from Leeds at Low Moor.

ABOVE: 10TH AUGUST, 1957. With the grim austerity of the post-war years receeding, the late 1950s saw millions of Britons heading off for summer holidays at the coast, invariably on a Saturday. With car ownership still at a very low level this annual mass movement of humanity over about half a dozen Saturdays a year inevitably had to be accommodated by British Railways, a task which severely stretched the resources of its locomotive departments.

On this particular day, Low Moor shed was so stretched that all it had left to work the 12 noon Sowerby Bridge to Bradford local was ex-Lancashire & Yorkshire 0-6-0 goods engine No. 52413, seen here approaching Bradford Exchange. Not only that, later in the day 52413 was put to work on the 3.30pm Liverpool Exchange to Leeds express which it took forward from Low Moor. These were the only occasions I ever saw one of these engines on a normal passenger train.

RIGHT: 25TH OCTOBER, 1957, 3.45PM. By 1957 the Compound 4-4-0s were reaching the end of the line but they still had the odd moment of glory in them.

No. 41068, of Holbeck shed, starts away from Leeds City North while assisting an overloaded 'Black Five' 4-6-0 on the southern leg of the Waverley from Edinburgh to London St. Pancras.

ABOVE: 12TH APRIL, 1958, 2.20PM. The 4-4-0 was the standard British passenger engine until replaced by bigger engines and, ultimately, by diesels. This once commonplace wheel arrangement was all but extinct by the early1960s but in 1958 Gresley's LNER D49 Hunts and Shires were still doing sterling work - if not for much longer. No. 62773 *The South Durham*, of Neville Hill shed(then 50B) was at Leeds City South preparing its stock for the 2.35pm local to Harrogate. It was one of the D49/2s with Lentz Rotary Cam poppet valve gear.

LEFT: 10TH MAY, 1958. Doncaster has always been a major attraction for enthusiasts and to some extent remains so to this day.

One of its attractions was the solitary W1 4-6-4 No. 60700 which rarely ventured north of the town. Here, the monster is ready to depart with the 10.8am for King's Cross.

Built at Darlington in 1929 as Gresley's experimental high pressure engine No. 10000, the so-called "Hush Hush," it was rebuilt as a conventional locomotive with A4 styling in 1937 but never carried a name. It was withdrawn in June, 1959.

ABOVE: 10TH MAY, 1958, 1.30PM. Contrasting sharply with the W1, D16 4-4-0 No. 62529 - whose lineage can be traced back to the famous Great Eastern Claud Hamiltons - stands in steam on Doncaster shed. Near the end of its life, it was a rare visitor and probably arrived from the GE area while deputising for a failed Sandringham or B16 4-6-0.

.

BELOW: 10TH JULY, 1958, 7PM. Another breed on its way out by the late 1950s was the 7F 0-8-0 introduced by Fowler for the LMS in 1929. No. 49627 was on Low Moor shed prior to working the evening Bradford Bridge Street to Aintree goods. This rather unsuccessful class originally consisted of 175 locos but by this time only 20 remained and they were rarely seen in the West Ridng.

ABOVE: 19TH AUGUST, 1958, 4.43PM. Lancaster had become a refuge for other sheds' unwanted and uncared for Compounds but a surprise arrival in summer, 1958 was very clean 41157. Officially allocated to Trafford Park, it was around for several weeks before moving to Derby for further use. Making a pleasing sight, it waits to leave Bradford Forster Square with the 5.10pm "Residential" to Morecambe which it will work as far as Skipton. By this time this was the last regular express passenger job for a Compound anywhere in Britain.

LEFT: 5TH APRIL, 1959. During 1959, bridge renewals in the Wortley/ Copley Hill area of Leeds caused the main King's Cross trains to run to and from Bradford Exchange via Wakefield Kirkgate, Cleckheaton and Low Moor instead of Leeds, with Leeds being served by portions attached and detached at Low Moor.

The result was the rare appearance of East Coast Pacifics at Bradford. A3 No. 60062 *Minoru* awaits departure with the 10.56am to King's Cross.

18.5.57: Ardsley's C13 4-4-2T 67427 deputises for an N1 on the 10.50am Bradford Ex.-King's Cross as far as Wakefield, gaining 2.5 mins. on the schedule.

5.4.58: Holbeck's veteran 2P 4-4-0 No. 40491 takes an 8-coach relief to the 12.15pm St. Pancras-Bradford forward from Leeds.

ABOVE: 11TH APRIL, 1959. 12 NOON. During the 1930s the Gresley N2 0-6-2T s had a spell in the Bradford area but, primarily intended for King's Cross area suburban services they normally only reached the West Riding for attention at Doncaster 'Plant' Works.
Wearing a Hatfield destination board, No. 69575 rests on Doncaster shed before returning to its home depot at King's Cross following light repairs at the 'Plant.' It is equipped with condensing apparatus and small chimney for working the Metropolitan lines to Moorgate.

BELOW: 18TH APRIL, 1959, 9.57AM . The baths and gardens of Harrogate may be a far cry from the steelworks of Sheffield but they were both in the old West Riding. One of Neville Hill's BR Standard 2-6-4Ts, No. 80118, awaits departure from Harrogate station with spa town's portion of the Yorkshire Pullman to King's Cross.

ABOVE: 22ND APRIL, 1959. Still on the Harrogate line, this time at Headingley on the outskirts of Leeds. K1 2-6-0 No. 62049 of 50A York shed approaches the station with a Leeds-bound weedkilling train. On the right is a loading dock used by visiting circus trains.

BELOW: 15TH JULY, 1959. This unusual view of Manningham shed yard shows three pre-grouping locos in store. Lancashire & Yorkshire Radial tank No. 50795 is accompanied by Midland 3F 0-6-0s Nos. 43784 and 43586. The 0-6-0s were repeatedly in and out of traffic but the Radial had not steamed since autumn, 1956. In accordance with the instructions for stored engines, 50795 was moved about the yard and even turned but she was towed away for scrap on 3rd November, 1959, by which time she was the last remaining member of this famous class in Yorkshire.
On the right is the oil gas works which produced gas for a variety of railway uses while the locos are standing on the site of the long-demolished straight shed.

ABOVE: 15TH AUGUST, 1959, 1.59PM. No. 61415, one of the North Eastern B16/1 4-6-0s designed by Sir Vincent Raven and built in September, 1920, has just been turned at Bradford Forster Square after arriving with the 1 1.5am from Scarborough.

RIGHT: 27TH AUGUST, 1959. The pre-grouping variety of the West Riding was considerably enhanced by the presence of the Great Northern J6 class 0-6-0s. Introduced by Gresley in 1911, they could still be seen on empty stock duty and even banking Deltic-hauled London trains out of Leeds Central as late as summer, 1962. No. 64268 is on more down to earth business at Laisterdyke, near Bradford, with a coal train for the nearby Birkshall gas works.

RIGHT: 12TH SEPTEMBER, 1959. Sheffield Darnall was a big steam depot but it would soon see a huge influx of diesels which in 1964 would all migrate to the new Tinsley diesel depot.

For the time being its allocation included the Parker N5 0-6-2Ts introduced in 1891 by the Manchester, Sheffield & Lincolnshire Railway, the forerunner of the Great Central. The first locos in the country to have Belpaire fireboxes, they were allocated to sheds all over the system. The end was nigh for this pair, 69290(at the back) was withdrawn the following month and 69314 in February, 1960.

BELOW: 12TH SEPTEMBER, 1959. The B17 4-6-0s were on the verge of extinction yet Ipswich-based 61637 *Thorpe Hall*, one of the original B17/1 class introduced by Gresley in 1928, was still on top link duty, having brought the Harwich-Liverpool boat train into Sheffield Victoria. No. 61637 must have been making one of its last ever journeys for within days of this photograph it was withdrawn and sent for scrap.

RIGHT: 30TH OCTOBER, 1959, 9.50AM. Bradford still enjoyed through services to three London stations in the 1950s: King's Cross, St. Pancras and Marylebone. The South Yorkshireman, at Bradford Exchange with B1 4-6-0 No. 61387 in charge went to Marylebone by way of Huddersfield, Sheffield Victoria and the Great Central main line. Alas, the gradual run-down of the GC line was about to start and the South Yorkshireman was axed within weeks of this photo being taken.

SHORT MEMORIES

27.5.58: J39 0-6-0 No. 64821 works a Whit. Tuesday 9-coach Knaresborough to Bradford relief via Wetherby.

10.1.59: J11 0-6-0 No. 64425 powers the 2.5pm Barnsley to Doncaster stopping passenger train.

LEFT: 31ST OCTOBER, 1959. The Huddersfield area possessed a network of short branch lines unrivalled elsewhere in the West Riding but their days were numbered even before Beeching had been appointed. Here, Ivatt Class 2 2-6-2T 41263 waits to leave Holmfirth with the 1.35pm to Huddersfield on the last day of passenger services. The Holmfirth branch closed altogether in May, 1965.

ABOVE: 21ST NOVEMBER, 1959. Apart from the great variety of its native locomotive stock, the West Riding received occasional allocations of alien engines from far-off parts of the network. In this instance, the late 1950s saw a number of Great Eastern 0-6-0Ts temporarily transferred north to Doncaster to overcome a shortage of shunting engines left by withdrawals of the elderly GN J52 0-6-0STs. J69 No. 68508, pictured by the old coaling stage at Doncaster shed, survived long enough to become the last GE loco in the West Riding, being withdrawn in February, 1961.

BELOW: 21ST NOVEMBER, 1959. In the melancholy lines of engines awaiting scrapping at Doncaster Works was B17/1 4-6-0 No. 61647 *Helmingham Hall*, just 24 years old but a victim of rapid dieselisation in East Anglia. She awaits her fate complete with nameplates, number plate, shedplate and works plates.

1960 - 1965

ABOVE: 5TH JANUARY, 1960, 12.6PM. A handful of GNR J52s made it into the 1960s and it seems incredible that over the next eight years the steam holocaust would see even the most modern engines, some little more than five years old, broken up for scrap. Sixty year-old 68834 was in its last month when shunting a trip working at Ardsley.

ABOVE: 21ST FEBRUARY, 1960. An operation which seems quite incredible nowadays when even locomotives are moved by road. WD 2-8-0 No. 90353 with the aid of a well wagon moved an entire signal box, intact, the short distance from Skellow to Adwick Junction on the West Riding & Grimsby line just north of Doncaster.

ABOVE: 27TH MARCH, 1960. Class O2/2 2-8-0 No. 63941 was on Doncaster shed receiving minor repairs to its motion. Rather oddly, the O2/2s, introduced by the LNER in 1924 retained the spartan Great Northern-style cabs while the older O2/1s, introduced by the GN in 1921 were all rebuilt with side window cabs.

BELOW: 27TH MARCH, 1960. The scrap line at Doncaster Works comprised an unusual mix of locomotives. With the remains of earlier victims scattered around them, were A2/2 Pacific 60501 *Cock o' the North* followed by Midland 2P 4-4-0 40582, Midland 3F 0-6-0s 43759 and 43665, J6 0-6-0 64180 and K3 2-6-0 61806. No. 60501 was a Thompson 1943 rebuild of Gresley's pioneer Class P2 2-8-2 built in 1934 for heavy duties in Scotland. The A2/2s were not a great success and were early victims of the diesels. The three Midland engines had come from Derby Works which could no longer cope with the mass onslaught of Midland and early LMS locos then being withdrawn. They were the first convoy of four locos a week to arrive at Doncaster for breaking up. Later on, LMR locos were sent direct from their depots to Doncaster.

RIGHT: 27TH MARCH, 1960, 4.5PM. Goole was the only shed in the West Riding with an allocation of Lancashire & Yorkshire Railway 'Pug' 0-4-0STs. Their short wheelbase and 21 ton weight made them ideal for working sharply curved dock lines and much difficulty was experienced finding suitable diesels to replace them. When this photograph was taken of 51222 at Goole shed with other familiar local power, she wasn't far short of her 60th birthday.

BELOW: 2ND APRIL, 1960. Seven of England's remaining ten Great Central D11/1 'Large Director' 4-4-0s were stored in the coal sidings at Darnall motive power depot. In the left row are 62666 *Zeebrugge,* 62662 *Prince of Wales* and 62668 *Jutland,* and on the right are 62669 *Ypres,* 62664 *Princess Mary,* 62667 *Somme* and 62660 *Butler Henderson.*

Among the most successful British 4-4-0s, their days were numbered but they were brought out of store to help with 1960 summer traffic before finally being consigned to the scrapheap or, thankfully in the case of 62660, preservation. Examples of the LNER-built D11/2 class survived in Scotland for about a year longer.

SHORT MEMORIES

2.4.60: Unrebuilt Patriot 45519 *Lady Godiva* from 82E Bristol Barrow Road heads the 2.31pm Sheffield-Leeds stopper.

23.7.60: B16/1 4-6-0 No. 61473 is on Sheffield Darnall shed.

22.11.60: Perth Jubilee 45673 *Keppel* heads the down Waverley past Apperley Bridge.

ABOVE: 2ND APRIL, 1960, 4PM. A candidate for the West Riding's oldest active BR steam loco, Canklow shed's Johnson 1F 0-6-0T No. 41875 on station pilot duty at Rotherham Masborough. This was one of no less than 179 new locomotives put into service by the Midland Railway in 1899. Sister 41708 was much older and although stored at Canklow when withdrawn in December, 1966, she was allocated outside the county when working.

BELOW: 16TH APRIL, 1960, 3.5PM. Unrebuilt Patriot 4-6-0 No. 45517 from Liverpool Bank Hall was no stranger to the West Riding but to see an unrebuilt Patriot on the Settle & Carlisle was rare indeed. A probable explanation for it being on the London-bound Waverley is that it had worked a Liverpool-Glasgow as far as Carlisle where it was requisitioned for the Waverley following failure of the booked engine. No. 45517 is seen going well past Hirst Woods where the driver had already shut off steam for the slack through Shipley.

ABOVE: 6TH MAY, 1960, 2.18PM. Q6 0-8-0 No. 63449 comes off its home shed at Neville Hill. These North Eastern goods engines became the last pre-grouping locomotives to work in the West Riding and along with their J27 0-6-0 sisters, the last in the country. No. 63449 was scrapped in 1963 but 63420 and 63426 worked at Normanton until October, 1966 when they were sent north to Tyne Dock for further use. Behind the Q6 are the long-gone Neville Hill carriage sheds and a J39 0-6-0, while an NE slotted signal stands guard on the left.

BELOW: 6TH MAY, 1960. Liverpool Bank Hall engines were regular power for Calder Valley line expresses between Yorkshire, Manchester and Liverpool. Ready to leave Leeds Central with the 5.10pm to Liverpool is 'Black Five' 44743, the last survivor of its class with Caprotti valve gear when withdrawn in January, 1966.

ABOVE: 28TH MAY, 1960, 1.54PM. Hellifield's 40685 was Yorkshire's last active 2P 4-4-0 when piloting Royal Scot 4-6-0 No. 46109 *Royal Engineer* through Bingley with the up Thames-Clyde Express. Why the 2P was assisting is unclear for the train was running early and the 2P blowing off so the Scot could not have been in too bad a state.

BELOW: 4TH JUNE, 1960. Gresley A3 Pacifics displaced from the East Coast main line had recently been assigned to principal Settle & Carlisle expresses and in less than an hour two variant's of the route's prime motive power had headed its named trains past Apperley Junction, where the Ilkley line parts company with the Leeds-Skipton line. At 2.24pm Royal Scot No. 46145 *The Duke of Wellington's Regt.(West Riding)* was storming past with the Edinburgh-bound Waverley.

ABOVE: 4TH JUNE, 1960, 3.19PM. The second variant, one of the recently-assigned A3s, 60088 *Book Law*, has the St. Pancras to Glasgow Thames-Clyde Express firmly under control.

Although putting up some exceptionally fine work on this route and being well liked by enginemen, the A3s were not officially considered a success, probably because they were a very tight fit on the Holbeck depot turntable and sometimes had to be turned on the already busy triangle at Leeds west end, as well as having to go to Farnley Junction for boiler washout and to Neville Hill for piston and valve examination.

BELOW: 4TH JUNE, 1960, 7.10PM. Little BR Standard Class 2 2-6-0 No. 78024 from Millhouses shed, Sheffield, was gallantly battling towards Apperley Bridge with 11-coaches on the down Devonian. Holbeck depot must have been desperately short of power to turn out such a small engine for such a big load but even so, she made it to Bradford.

OSMONDTHORPE. WHIT. MONDAY 6th JUNE, 1960. The next four pictures at this east Leeds location show the variety of additional passenger trains to be seen in a short space of time on a bank holiday in the early 1960s. Seven steam-hauled excursions passed Osmondthorpe that morning, four hauled by the handsome B16/1s. They were the heaviest trains yet the elderly NER 4-6-0s completely outclassed the other locomotives. ABOVE: 10.1am . Thompson B1 4-6-0 No. 61035 *Pronghorn* has just passed Neville Hill depot and is digging into the 1 in 153/162 climb to Cross Gates with a Leeds-Whitby excursion.

BELOW: At 10.14am.,Gresley K3 2-6-0 No. 61965 heads east with a Leeds-York excursion.

ABOVE: At 11.5am came B16/1 No. 61471 with a Leeds-Scarborough excursion, completely outperforming the other classes despite being in her 40th year of service.

BELOW: On its way out of Leeds at 12.4pm was this Wetherby races special double headed by one of Neville Hill's BR Standard Class 4 2-6-4Ts, No. 80119, and LMS 4F 0-6-0 No. 44477 of Sheffield Grimesthorpe. The 4F had struggled manfully as far as Leeds with the heavy train from Heeley(just south of Sheffield) but it was considered prudent to provide the youthful assisting engine for the difficult run between Cross Gates and Wetherby. No. 80119 was just six years old whereas 44477 was in its 33rd year.

ABOVE: 9TH JUNE, 1960, 3.31PM.   Besides Doncaster, Selby was the other principal West Riding station where the East Coast main line Pacifics could be seen heading Anglo-Scottish expresses. But with the Deltics poised to make their appearance, 1960 was the penultimate year in which steam would have a major presence on such top link work. Here, York-based Thompson A2/3 No. 60512 *Steady Aim* rumbles over the River Ouse swing bridge and takes the station through road with the 7.5am Aberdeen-King's Cross.

BELOW: 9TH JUNE, 1960, 7.46PM. Gresley A4 No. 60034 *Lord Farringdon* was accelerating through Selby station with the up afternoon Talisman. The DMU on the right was on Goole branch line service.

ABOVE: 15TH JUNE, 1960. The rarest engine I ever saw at Laisterdyke was pioneer Patriot No. 45500 *Patriot*, hauling an 11-coach empty stock train out of Planetrees carriage sidings. I was very pleased with my luck because, supposedly practising for a school cross-country run, I just happened to have my camera with me.

BELOW: 18TH JUNE, 1960, 11.40AM. A fine vista of Bradford Bridge Street goods yards and the "Lancashire & Yorkshire Ry Goods Warehouse" being shunted by 3F 0-6-0T No. 47635. The variety of traffic includes tractors on low-sided wagons. Despite its busy air, Bridge Street closed completely on 20th October, 1962 and in the 1970s the site was transformed into the Transport Interchange.

ABOVE: 20TH JUNE, 1960. After the demise of the Compounds, various types of 2-6-0s were tried on the Morecambe trains and here BR Standard Class 4 No. 76051 accelerates through Manningham with the 5.10pm "Residential" from Bradford Forster Square. Built at Doncaster less than four years ago, she spent almost all her short working life at Kirkby Stephen, being transferred to Lancaster only weeks before this picture.

BELOW: 25TH JUNE, 1960. Contrasting with the above, 1921-vintage Midland 4F 0-6-0 No. 43945 from Heaton Mersey shed, Stockport, hurries through Laisterdyke station with the 3.55pm Leeds Central-Manchester Victoria which ran express to Halifax and avoided Bradford by using the Laisterdyke-Bowling line. The house above the retaining wall is all that remains of Laisterdyke station in 2003.

ABOVE: 25TH JUNE, 1960, 5.16PM. Another veteran on express passenger duty. Great Northern J6 0-6-0 No. 64277, built in 1922, has an easy load with the Bradford portion of the 12.40pm from King's Cross, seen passing Drighlington & Adwalton. When her time came, 64277 went out in style, being hauled to her fate at Doncaster Works on 15th June, 1962 by nothing less than A4 Pacific *Lord Farringdon*.

BELOW: 5TH JULY, 1960, 7.17PM. An even older 0-6-0, Midland 3F No. 43784 was working an evening transfer freight to Bradford Valley past Manningham Sidings box, the fourth wagon conveying a road roller.
No. 43784 belonged to a small class of engines built at Derby between the Johnson and Fowler eras which were referred to as Deeley 3Fs. However, this loco was by no means the first of the class yet it left Derby new in December, 1903, the month before Richard Mountford Deeley took office. Having been in and out of store depending on traffic requirements it was finally withdrawn three months later in October, 1960.

ABOVE: 9TH JULY, 1960. The exploits of the BR 9F 2-10-0 goods engines on express passenger trains are well known. In 1958 when barely run-in from new, some were achieving speeds in the 70s and 80s with sustained mile-a-minute running on both the Great Central and Great Northern main lines. The whole affair culminated with 92184 reaching 90mph down Stoke bank in August of that year, and when news of this reached the authorities the instruction came from on high, maybe from within the hallowed walls of 222 Marylebone Road itself, that the practice must stop immediately.

Here, Saltley's No. 92137 is working the 11-coach 11.5am Filey Holiday Camp-Manchester express up the 1 in 105 through Slaithwaite with consummate ease. There was no chance of any high speed exploits on this tortuous route, but a high speed turnround ensued in Manchester for in less than two hours she was heading back towards Leeds with the 13-coach 5.37pm Manchester-Newcastle express.

LEFT: 23RD JULY, 1960. Fine engines they may have been but in BR days the Robinson Great Central 2-8-0s were often so filthy it was virtually impossible to read their numbers which makes this view such a rarity. Class 04/3 No. 63846 was obviously ex-works when on her home depot at Sheffield Darnall. One of 521 built for the Railway Operating Division for first world war service overseas, she was one of 273 bought by the LNER after repatriation and lasted well into the final years of steam. Doncaster-based sister 63764 survived until February, 1966, becoming the last GC locomotive in the West Riding.

ABOVE: 23RD JULY, 1960, 12.47PM. One of England's last active Gresley K2 2-6-0s, No. 61728 runs "under the wires" as it approaches Darnall station with the 12.41pm Sheffield Victoria to Nottingham Victoria stopping train. On the left, O4/8 2-8-0 No. 63645 shunts wagons of coal into the motive power depot yard while on the right are the works of Cravens, the carriage and wagon builders.

BELOW: 23RD JULY, 1960, 1.20PM. Coming the other way under the 1500 volt dc catenery was BR Standard Class 7 Britannia Pacific No. 70003 *John Bunyan* on the Harwich-Liverpool boat train. Still allocated to Norwich, 70003 was among the East Anglian Britannias which ousted the Sandringham 4-6-0s from this service after themselves being displaced from the Great Eastern main line by diesels.

LEFT: 23RD JULY, 1960, 4.38PM. With the motive power departments under great strain on summer Saturdays, all kinds of engines could turn up on all kinds of workings and the Sheffield-Leeds stopping service could produce just about anything. In this case, it was Rugby's unrebuilt Patriot 4-6-0 No. 45541 *Duke of Sutherland* which was leaving Rotherham Masborough with the 4.15pm from Sheffield to Leeds.

BELOW: 23RD JULY, 1960, 4.55PM. Probably the oldest active BR steam locomotive in the West Riding at the time was Canklow's 2F 0-6-0 No. 58170, built by Neilson & Co. for the Midland Railway in 1876. It acquired a Belpaire firebox and new cab in 1917 but everything else was original. The axle loading of under 13 tons was probably the reason for its longevity. It was rolling gently through Rotherham Masborough with a brake van while on its way home after trip working around the area's numerous small yards and sidings.

ABOVE: 18TH SEPTEMBER, 1960, 4.53PM.   In Manningham roundhouse were one of the depot's three 350hp diesel shunters, Carlisle Kingmoor 'Black Five' 44792(a regular visitor), 'Crab' 2-6-0 No. 42762 - a Manningham engine since at least 1945 - and 4-4-0 No. 41063, the last Compound in North Eastern Region stock. Last used in summer, 1958, it spent the following winter dumped outside and then in spring, 1959 was suprisingly greased and with sacking over the chimney brought into the shed where it stayed before being towed away in October, 1960 to Doncaster Works for immediate cutting up. But for this it could have been the longest-lived Compound. Instead, at 36 years and 3 months it had to make do with second place.

BELOW: 4TH JANUARY, 1961. Class O4/1 No. 63605, one of the elegant Great Central Robinson 2-8-0s - introduced in 1911 and nicknamed "Tinies" because of what was then considered to be their huge size - leaves Ardsley Old Coal Yard bang on time with the 2.10pm freight to York.

ABOVE: 3RD APRIL, 1961, 12 NOON. Displaced by West Coast main line electrification, several Royal Scots were transferred to the Midland line where they greatly improved the service, eliminating much of the expensive double-heading. Here, 46162 *Queen's Westminster Riflemen* from London's Kentish Town shed approaches Rotherham Masborough with the 10.30am Bradford Forster Square-St. Pancras during what was supposed to be the last fortnight of steam on these services. As described in *Drama and Decline,* this proved a total farce.

BELOW: 16TH JULY, 1961, 3.45PM. The Great Central was renowned for the quality build of its locomotives as this scene proves. Although their days were numbered, each of these J11 0-6-0s, Nos. 64377, 64442 and 64406 in steam at Mexborough shed, was around 55 years old. The coaling plant in the background was a different story. Built in 1961 as the last new plant for BR, it was declared redundant and demolished just four years later.

ABOVE: 27TH JULY, 1961, 9.45AM. The LMS Fowler Class 4 2-6-4Ts were a prominent feature of West Riding local passenger workings, especially in the area now known as West Yorkshire. No. 42384, one of those with the original open sided cab, accelerates through Laisterdyke West Junction after coming off the Bowling line with the Leeds portion of the 7am express from Southport which it worked from Low Moor.

BELOW: 27TH JULY, 1961, 9.58AM. Shortly after 42384 had passed came this juicy scene involving Gresley 0-6-0s from two different eras. Great Northern J6 No. 64203, built 1913, heads an Ardsley to Bradford goods while LNER J39 No. 64872, 15 years its junior, leads an engineers' crane away from Bradford.

31.12.60: The last weekend of trans-Pennine steam sees Jubilees 45660 *Rooke* and 45735 *Comet* (a class 7P rebuild) double head the 5pm Liverpool-Newcastle.

17.6.61: 4F 0-6-0 No. 44353 of Northampton works the 1.18pm King's Cross-Bradford from Wakefield.

ABOVE: 31ST JULY, 1961, 8.33PM. Manningham 3F 0-6-0 No. 43586 was still going strong and benefitting from unofficial lining on the splashers. Built for the Midland Railway by Kitson & Co. in 1899, her last claim to fame before withdrawal in August, 1962 came on 23rd June, 1962 when she worked the last BR passenger train on the Worth Valley line.

BELOW: 4TH AUGUST, 1961, 2.25PM. Totally steam-tight BR Standard Class 5 4-6-0 No. 73132 from Patricroft shed and one of 30 such locos equipped with Caprotti valve gear, accelerates vigorously away from the Shipley slack with the 1.54pm Leeds-Morecambe and Carnforth express.

Experience with the Caprotti 'Black Fives' revealed worthwhile savings in coal consumption and double the mileage between piston and valve examinations. Any further steam locomotive development would almost certainly have seen any high-powered high-mileage locomotives fitted with Caprotti poppet valve gear.

ABOVE: 5TH AUGUST, 1961, 10.18AM. One of the Ivatt Caprotti 'Black Fives' referred to on the previous page barks up the grade through Slaithwaite with the 9.3am Leeds-Llandudno. In this case, however, Llandudno Junction-based 44742 is certainly not steam-tight.

BELOW: 7TH AUGUST, 1961, 8.33AM. By the end of 1962 the entire class of 192 K3 2-6-0s had gone. No. 61975, briefly allocated to Low Moor to help with the summer rush, puts on a brave show while passing Luddendenfoot station on the Calder Valley line with the 7.50am Bradford-Blackpool August bank holiday excursion. The locomotive was withdrawn the following month.

ABOVE: 12TH AUGUST, 1961, 10.28AM. Hull Dairycoates depot had a long association with the K3s which it used on important fish trains. No. 61871 remained there to the end, unlike some members of the class which wandered around "job seeking" in their final years. Here, she climbs through Cross Gates with the summer Saturday 8.50am Stalybridge-Scarborough. The through roads have long since been removed.

BELOW: 12TH AUGUST, 1961, 12.37PM. Royston-based Stanier Class 3 2-6-2T No. 40193 brings the 12.15pm Leeds-Cudworth stopping train composed of an interesting mix of coaches into Normanton station.
Anyone who has seen Normanton station in 2003 will be hard pressed to believe it is the same place as this. All the extensive railway layout has gone except two running lines and the island platform which is mostly covered by a shrubbery.

ABOVE: 12TH AUGUST, 1961, 1.1PM. Bank Hall Jubilee 4-6-0 No. 45698 *Mars* passes a WD 2-8-0 as it pulls away from the Normanton stop with the 10.30am Liverpool Exchange-York express.

BELOW: 23RD OCTOBER, 1961, 2.29PM. With the GN Queensbury line closed as a through route from May, 1955, coal traffic between the south side of Bradford and Airedale had to make a lengthy detour via Idle to Shipley where it then reversed before taking the Aire Valley line. At least it brought a bit of variety for the motive power was usually a Low Moor J39 and occasionally a J6. Here, J39 No. 64886 makes an almighty pace through Crossflatts with the 1pm Bradford Quarry Gap-Skipton Through Freight. The train has the Fast line and the crew seem determined to prove that their LNER J39 is every bit as good as the native 4Fs.

ABOVE: 26TH OCTOBER, 1961, 4.48PM. Midland 4F 0-6-0 No. 43906 from Royston shed blasts past Mirfield station while heading the 2.25pm Carlton-Rose Grove class J coal train. Examples of the American-style colour light speed signalling system installed on this stretch of line by the LMS in the 1930s can be seen just beyond the platform end.
No. 43906 retained 'LMS' on its tender with the BR lion and wheel plastered over the 'M' at least until 1964. Built at Derby in 1920, this engine and sister 43968 were the last Midland Railway locomotives allocated to a West Riding depot when withdrawn in November, 1965.

BELOW: 11TH NOVEMBER, 1961. The reliability of the new main line diesels was so bad that Neville Hill depot was required to keep an A3 Pacific standby "in good nick" ready to take over at a moment's notice. On this day spotless No. 60074 *Harvester* was the standby, keeping company with grubby K1 2-6-0 No. 62057 and a number of idle 'Peaks' skulking on the site of a demolished part of the steam roundhouse.

LEFT: 18TH NOVEMBER, 1961, 1 1. 57AM. Waiting the road twixt the station and the goods warehouse at Wakefield Kirkgate were Stanier Class 4 2-6-4T No. 42650, K3 2-6-0 No. 61984 and B1 No. 61040 *Roedeer*. The first two engines are running light, presumably from the shed and only the B1 is attached to the crane.

SHORT MEMORIES

12.11.60: The following are noted passing Calverley & Rodley: Britannia 70053 *Moray Firth* on the down Waverley, Royal Scot 46130 *The West Yorkshire Regiment* on the up Thames-Clyde, A3 60080 *Dick Turpin* on the down Thames-Clyde and A3 60084 *Trigo* on the up Waverley.

RIGHT: 9TH DECEMBER, 1961, 12.44PM. I couldn't believe my eyes when Patricroft 'Super D' 0-8-0 No. 49199 emerged from the mist at Skipton station with empties from Barrow to Manvers Main. These were now the only London & North Western engines to be seen in the West Riding and by this time their appearances were decidedly rare.

ABOVE: 2ND MARCH, 1962, 6.17PM. The 5.28pm Leeds City North-Ilkley was most interesting for it was one of the very few steam passenger trains in Wharfedale and it ran via Horsforth, Athington and Otley. It was as much a parcels train and is seen here unloading after arriving at Ilkley behind Holbeck's double-chimnied Caprotti 'Black Five' No. 44756.

BELOW: 10TH MARCH, 1962, 3.15PM. My candidate for the oldest active Midland Railway locomotive allocated to the West Riding by this time was Hellifield's 63 year-old 3F 0-6-0 No. 43585, seen alongside her home depot while shunting stock off the 2.20pm passenger train from Blackburn. As station pilot, she proudly displays class A headlamps.

RIGHT: 17TH MARCH, 1962, 10.52AM. It was another day when the diagrammed Type 4 diesel wasn't available for the Bradford-Paignton Devonian so Holbeck Jubilee 45569 *Tasmania* stepped in to fill the breach. She makes an impressive sight when setting off from Sheffield Midland.

BELOW: 18TH MARCH, 1962, 2.50PM. Yet another day when workable diesels were in short supply. Royal Scot 46127 *Old Contemptibles* from Crewe North stands by the diesel fuelling point at Holbeck while preparing to take over the up Thames-Clyde Express. Britannia Pacific No. 70054 *Dornoch Firth* waits behind while Peak D135 sits alongside.

SHORT MEMORIES

12.5.62: Low Moor Royal scot 46130 works the 8.50am Leeds-St. Pancras while deputising for a diesel.

ABOVE: 28TH MARCH, 1962, 9.45AM. By February, Yorkshire's last four Lancashire & Yorkshire 'A' class 0-6-0s - by now the last L&Y locos in the county - were at Sowerby Bridge. The oldest, 52121 built at Horwich in May, 1891, had only received an Intermediate Repair in 1959 and was smartly turned out when arriving at Greetland to take up pilot duty. She was the West Riding's oldest active L&Y engine by the time she was withdrawn in November and, being mostly as built, arguably the oldest active BR steam loco allocated to the West Riding.

BELOW: 13TH APRIL, 1962, 9.58AM. Great Northern J50 0-6-0T No.68965 was sent briefly to Mirfield for trials. Seen shunting a trip working at Cleckheaton Central, it was considered unsuitable and returned to its native Ardsley to be replaced by J39s.

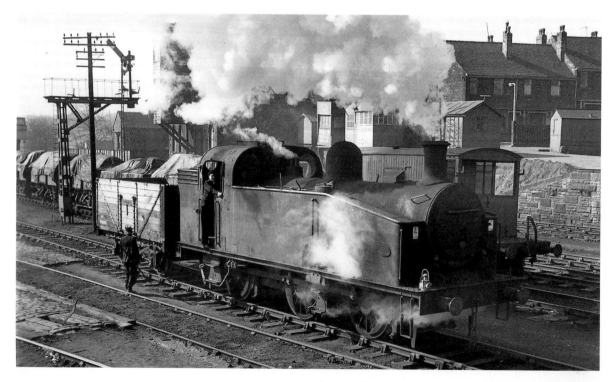

ABOVE: 14TH APRIL, 1962, 6.9PM. 'Crab' 2-6-0 No. 42851 makes a fine sight in the spring sunlight as it pulls out of Bingley with the 5.42pm Leeds-Morecambe stopper. The goods yard on the right closed in June, 1965.

BELOW: 21ST APRIL, 1962, 11.23AM. In early 1962 some of the last remaining unrebuilt Patriot 4-6-0s were transferred to Lancaster to help out on the Morecambe-Leeds and Bradford trains, but within months all had been withdrawn. Nevertheless, for a short time their graceful lines greatly enhanced the scene. Un-named 45510 roars through Steeton & Silsden with the 10.47am Leeds-Morecambe and Carnforth.

ABOVE: 21ST APRIL, 1962, 7.20PM. Stanier 2-6-0s normally came only from the Diggle or Calder Valley direction so 42963 of Crewe South was a rare visitor to Keighley when heading a football special returning from Sheffield to Burnley. The Midland signal box, semaphores, bay platform line, water column and private siding going to the left were all points of interest which no longer exist on this, the main line half of the station.

LEFT: 23RD APRIL, 1962, 8.50PM. 'Crab' 2-6-0 No. 42705 rests beneath the gas lights at Bradford Exchange after bringing in the 7.5pm Easter Monday relief from Manchester Victoria. Engine and crew had made a magnificent run with the 10-coach train until a diesel multiple unit was allowed to go in front of them from Halifax.

Gas lighting was used at Bradford Exchange until 1964.

RIGHT: 30TH APRIL, 1962. The 7.25pm Bradford Bridge Street-Huddersfield Hillhouse fitted freight regularly loaded to 600 tons and was double-headed to Low Moor. The assisting engine was always a WD 2-8-0 but the train engine was anything Low Moor shed had available. This was the most bizarre combination I ever saw: Royal Scot No. 46109 *Royal Engineer* and WD No. 90397.

The train was regularly stopped at Coal Shoots box to let the 7.30 Bradford-Liverpool DMU pass and the crews then had the unenviable task of restarting the mammoth load on the 1 in 50 bank and over the crossover with resulting fireworks.

By this time the Royal Scots were something of a mystery. Displaced from Holbeck by diesels in September, 1961 all five went to Low Moor but three were soon passed on to Mirfield. As express passenger engines they were unsuited to freight and I do wonder if they formed an unofficial pool of diesel standbys for they kept appearing at Glasgow, Carlisle and St. Pancras deputising for failed 'Peaks'. This view is strengthened by the fact that in June, 1962 all five returned to Holbeck.

BELOW: 19TH MAY, 1962, 2.14PM. The south end of Sheffield Midland. Jubilee No. 45639 *Raleigh* makes a rousing start with the 12.52pm York-Bristol while deputising for a Type 4 diesel. Having arrived three minutes early, it was delayed by the need to take water. Behind Sheffield South No.2 box is diesel standby, fellow Jubilee No. 45620 *North Borneo* while Standard 2-6-0 No. 78027 waits to work a Chinley local. In less than half a mile the start from Sheffield Midland took trains on to a 1 in 100 ascent that continued without a break for five and a half miles to Bradway Tunnel. Consequently, steam departures were lively and sometimes volcanic.

ABOVE; 11TH JUNE, 1962. Drafted in to help with bank holiday traffic, Stourton 8F 2-8-0 No. 48084 pulls out from under Leeds City's 93 year-old Victorian roof with the 11.45am Whit Monday races special to Wetherby. Over the next 40 years the station would be totally rebuilt and totally rebuilt again, the latest 21st Century trainshed recapturing the imposing style of the original and thankfully replacing the miserable 1960s version.

BELOW: 12TH JUNE, 1962, 1 1.23AM. Jubilee No. 45656 *Cochrane* roars up through Millhouses with the 8.5am Newcastle-Birmingham relief loaded to 13 bogies. The first four coaches are obviously "strengtheners" added at Sheffield. The immaculate condition of the locomotive is of note for it was a local Millhouses engine till that depot closed on 1st January, 1962 when it was sent to Canklow, almost certainly for storage. In the same month as this picture it was transferred to Darnall for use on summer traffic. Even so, it was condemned four months later. Note too that it still carries a 41C Millhouses shedplate.

ABOVE: 23RD JUNE, 1962, 8.11AM. The 7.26am Cudworth to Leeds was a fascinating train. It was one of the few remaining steam-hauled local passenger trains, ran to "accelerated timings" and was booked Mondays to Saturdays for a Royston 4F 0-6-0 goods engine. Timekeeping was exemplary and the whole affair was a bit of a time warp. Here, No. 44099 arrives at Leeds City North ahead of time.

BELOW: 23RD JUNE, 1962, 10.26AM. In this splendid view of Rotherham Masborough, York V2 No. 60941 prepares to hand over the 7.30 Newcastle-Paignton to a London Midland loco which will avoid Sheffield by taking the train forward via the "Old Road" through Canklow and Barrow Hill.

ABOVE: 23RD JUNE, 1962, 2.2PM. York B16/2 4-6-0 No. 61435 heads through Brightside, just north of Sheffield, with the 10.35am Scarborough to Derby which it is working as far as Sheffield Midland. The B16/2s were Gresley rebuilds of the B16/1s introduced in 1937 with Walschaerts valve gear on the outside cylinders, derived motion on the inside cylinder and right hand drive. No. 61435 became the last B16 of all, being officially withdrawn in July, 1964 but tragically it eluded preservation.

BELOW: 22ND JULY, 1962, 2.32PM. Having put up exceptionally high mileages while deputising for English Electric Type 4 diesels on the East Coast main line, A3 Pacifics 60067 *Ladas* and 60039 *Sandwich* were to be found in the boiler test shop at Doncaster Works. No. 60067 never left the works again but 60039 was out-shopped and continued to give sterling service.

ABOVE: 18TH AUGUST, 1962, 3PM. By 1962, bank holiday and summer Saturdays were just about the only time to see steam-hauled passenger trains on the Calder Valley main line, DMUs having taken over most of the normal passenger services in January. Here, Agecroft shed's 'Black Five' No. 45195 romps up to Summit Tunnel with the 11.32am Scarborough-Manchester.

BELOW: 29TH AUGUST, 1962, 7.20PM. Late in 1961, a number of redundant Thompson L1 2-6-4T s were transferred to Ardsley and Low Moor sheds as replacements for ageing J50 0-6-0Ts. Their long wheelbase caused frequent derailments in yards and sidings and they spent more time on passenger and parcels duties. No. 67721 pulls out of Bradford Exchange with the evening parcels train to Rochdale which includes a 4-wheeled vehicle reminiscent of a Hornby gauge '0' tinplate carriage.

ABOVE: 30TH AUGUST, 1962, 9.40AM. L1 No. 67721 on local trip work, this time at Laisterdyke East yard. This engine was delivered new from Darlington Works to Hull Botanic Gardens depot on 25th May, 1948 but by the end of 1962 the entire class of 100 engines had been withdrawn.

BELOW: 30TH AUGUST, 1962, 10.12AM. Fairburn Class 4 2-6-4T No. 42109 makes rather heavy going through Laisterdyke station with the Bradford portion of the up Yorkshire Pullman.

ABOVE: 7TH SEPTEMBER, 1962, 9.13AM. Low Moor is another one of those places where today's empty space belies its past as an important railway centre. No. 42410, one of the Fowler 2-6-4Ts with a side window cab, hurries the 9.3am Halifax-King's Cross round the curve past the motive power depot. This was the penultimate day on which the train ran via Bradford.

BELOW: 17TH SEPTEMBER, 1962, 10.52AM. Someone at Low Moor shed had developed a nack for cleaning up the most unlikely engines for spotless J39s were indeed rare. No. 64918 compensates by smoking out the signalmen at elevated Laisterdyke West box while hauling wagons bound for Birkshall gas works.

ABOVE: 22ND SEPTEMBER, 1962, 8.35AM. The Laisterdyke-Shipley line through Idle lost its regular passenger service as long ago as 1931 but like many which remained open for freight, it still saw occasional excursion trains. With Fairburn tank 42107 and Black Five 44951 in charge, the 8.25am Idle to Blackpool approaches Eccleshill station. The prospect of any use by passenger trains ended when the Laisterdyke-Idle section closed completely on 31st October, 1964.

BELOW: 23RD SEPTEMBER, 1962, 2.15PM. A surprise inmate at Doncaster Works was withdrawn Great Eastern J17 0-6-0 65567, late of March shed. Built at Stratford Works in 1905, it had been chosen for inclusion in the National Collection and was at the 'Plant' for cosmetic restoration to original condition as GER No.1217.

RIGHT: 23RD SEPTEMBER, 1962, 2.20PM. A3 Pacific No. 60050 *Persimmon*, seen inside the main erecting shop at Doncaster Works, was one of those A3s intended for withdrawal as being redundant but which had to be put through works because of the poor availability of their diesel replacements.
Some sources indicate this locomotive as actually being scrapped by the date this photograph was taken.

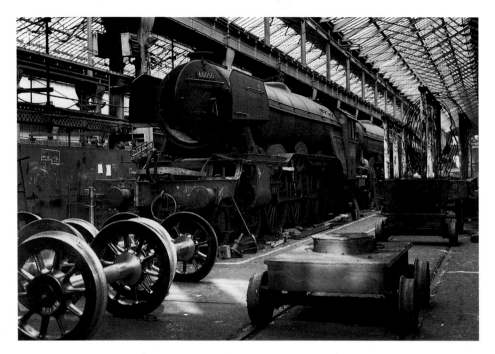

BELOW: 27TH SEPTEMBER, 1962. One of the classic West Riding 0-6-0 tank engines was the J50 with 71 out the 102 total once allocated to West Riding sheds. Introduced by the GNR in 1922 more were built by the LNER and some earlier J51s rebuilt as J50s. Very powerful engines for their size, they were classified 4F. One of the GN originals, No. 68922, pulls across Laisterdyke West Junction with the 12.30pm transfer freight from Birkshall gasworks to Laisterdyke East yard.

ABOVE: 29TH SEPTEMBER, 1962, 8AM. The Halifax Railfans Club ran a memorable railtour from Sowerby Bridge to Doncaster and Darlington Works - including over 120 miles on the East Coast main line - using L&Y 0-6-0 No. 52515 and 4F No. 44408 for a fare of £1 8s 6d. The locos are seen being prepared at Sowerby Bridge shed. The original plan was to use J6 No. 64277 with 52515 but the authorities got cold feet and withdrew the last three J6s in June, breaking them up the same month so the 4F was co-opted from Normanton shed as substitute for the GN loco. There was no problem with 52515 being fit for the marathon - despite her advancing years she had received a general repair and repaint at Horwich Works as late as November, 1961.

BELOW: 29TH SEPTEMBER, 1962, 9.57AM. The two 0-6-0s begin their expedition from Sowerby Bridge station, 27 minutes late.

ABOVE: 17TH OCTOBER, 1962, 9.52AM. After the South Yorkshireman was withdrawn, various routes were tried for replacement Halifax-London services. This train, pulling out of Barnsley Exchange with 'Black Five' 44951 in charge, is the 8.48am Halifax-St. Pancras which combined at Sheffield Midland with the main train from Leeds and Bradford Forster Square. Right of the station is the site of the loco depot, closed in January, 1960, the shed being demolished to make way for the new platform from which the train is departing. Before that Exchange only had one platform. Up on the left is Court House station, used only for parcels since 1960.

BELOW: 3RD NOVEMBER, 1962, 9.6AM. For a time Halifax enjoyed two London departures within 14 minutes of each other - the 8.48am to St. Pancras and 9.2am to King's Cross. Huddersfield Fowler 2-6-4T 42310 cruises over the River Calder and down towards Greetland with the King's Cross train which it will work via Huddersfield to Wakefield for combining with the main train from Leeds.

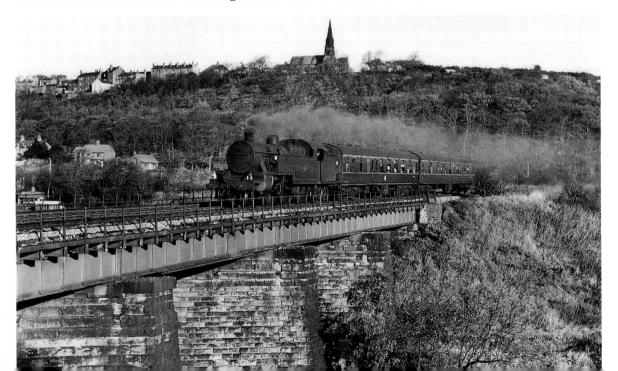

ABOVE: 24TH NOVEMBER, 1962, 10.10AM. In the final month of its short 13-year life, Colwick's L1 2-6-4T No. 67770 pilots Annesley 'Black Five' No. 45116 at Sheffield Victoria on the 10.18 stopping train to Nottingham.

BELOW: 19TH DECEMBER, 1962, 10.32AM. BR Standard locos were never allocated in great numbers to the West Riding and perhaps the rarest of all were the Class 3 2-6-2Ts. Only one, No. 82026 was ever allocated there, spending just four months at Low Moor and six months at Copley Hill before migrating south to Guildford. Viewed from the long-gone station platform, it is going on Low Moor shed during the first days of its service there which saw it used on Bradford-Penistone trains during a DMU shortage caused by fires on the new Calder Valley sets.

ABOVE: 22ND DECEMBER, 1962, 1.58PM. Closer to the northern reaches of the West Riding. Carlisle Kingmoor 'Black Five' No. 44903 hurries through Settle station with the 12.40pm Carlisle-Leeds Christmas extra.
In 2003, little of this view had changed. The crossover and semaphore signals had gone and a Midland Railway footbridge had been installed in the foreground, but it was still possible to see a steam-hauled express thunder through the station on its way south from Carlisle.

BELOW: 26TH JANUARY, 1963, 11.55AM. Signs of the tough winter to come - a winter so cold that it put many of the new diesels out of action with steam again coming to the rescue. King's Cross V2 No. 60854 leaves freezing Wakefield Westgate with a down express parcels train. Despite the engine's smart appearance, it was withdrawn but six months later.

SHORT MEMORIES

19.1.63: Notice at Bradford Forster Square: "It is regretted that owing to a defect in the heating apparatus on some diesel multiple unit trains, certain services are being worked by steam trains. The units are being modified as quickly as possible and will be back in service within a few days."

LEFT: 12TH FEBRUARY, 1963, 3.20PM. The new order at Leeds Central: Deltic No. D9015 *Tulyar* waits to work the down Queen of Scots Pullman as A3 No. 60062 *Minoru* takes care of the up White Rose.

BELOW: 16TH FEBRUARY, 1963, 2.15PM. A Christmas card scene at Steeton & Silsden it may be, but we're right in the thick of the most severe winter for at least 16 years. Snowdrifts completely block the Grassington branch and Holbeck 8F No. 48158 carrying class A head-lamps is going to the rescue with two large snowploughs.

ABOVE: 1ST MARCH, 1963, 1.31PM. Manningham 's Fairburn tanks could be called upon to haul monumental loads between Leeds City and Bradford Forster Square. No. 42093 recovers from a signal check as it approaches Forster Square with the 11-coach 7.35am express from Bristol.

BELOW: 2ND MARCH, 1963, 3.31PM. Withdrawal of the illustrious A4 Pacifics had begun and although steam was disappearing from the East Coast main line, it was still putting in some good work. Rather grubby King's Cross A4 No. 60029 *Woodcock* had arrived in Leeds while deputising for a Deltic on the down White Rose and, after a turnround of just two and a half hours, it was climbing strongly past Wortley South Jn. with the up train. Copley Hill MPD is beyond the signal box while the lines coming in from the left are the Wortley curve which provided a direct route to Bradford.

ABOVE: 23RD MARCH, 1963, 10.15AM. On the Huddersfield Newtown branch, the 9P96 10.10 Newtown to Hillhouse trip is propelled, brakevan leading, by Fowler 2-6-4T No. 42406 up towards the junction with the Huddersfield-Leeds main line at Red Doles where it will have to reverse.

BELOW: 23RD MARCH, 1963, 2.35PM. Withdrawn steam locomotives are starting to appear at depots around the country in increasing numbers. Heading the Bradford portion of the 10.20am from King's Cross, Fairburn 2-6-4T No. 42150 hurries past a line of withdrawn J39s and A3 No. 60069 *Sceptre* at Ardsley shed.

ABOVE: 31ST MAY, 1963. The coming of the 1955 Modernisation Plan meant that only 10 of the 25 BR Standard Clan Pacifics authorised were actually built but they were fairly frequent visitors to the West Riding, especially with Carlisle-Bradford trains. No. 72008 *Clan Macleod,* one of the batch allocated to Carlisle Kingmoor, leaves Bradford Forster Square with the 3.40pm stopper to Carlisle. All these engines were ultimately scrapped but in the 21st Century a project is under way to build an eleventh Clan, No. 72010 *Hengist.*

Major changes at Forster Square during the 1990s saw electrification, through services to and from King's Cross, a new station occupying the foreground, and the expanse of railway accommodating 72008 and beyond done away with and turned into a retail park.

BELOW: 15TH JUNE, 1963, 9.3AM. The weather is appropriately gloomy for the weekend which saw the official end of rostered steam-hauled passenger trains on the East Coast main line. On the penultimate day, A3 No. 60107 *Royal Lancer* arrives at Leeds Central with the 4am from King's Cross - which was as much a parcels train as a passenger service, hence the five-hour journey time. *Royal Lancer* was built at Doncaster in May, 1923 and during its 40 years service ran over 2.25 million miles, true value for money.

ABOVE: 15TH JUNE, 1963. J50 0-6-0T No. 68892, a 1929 LNER rebuild from a 1914-built GN Class J51, pushes loaded coal wagons up the steep incline to the coaling stage at Copley Hill shed. Like 68922 on page 67, this J50 was withdrawn in September, 1963. Depending on one's attitude towards rebuilding, 68892 or 68922 was by this time the oldest Great Northern engine in revenue-earning service in the West Riding. J50s were still in departmental use as Doncaster Works shunters.

BELOW: 5TH JULY, 1963. A Bradford Valley-Lancaster freight has derailed at Shipley Bradford Junction, spreading itself across all four passenger lines. The Wakefield steam breakdown crane brought by York K1 62046 has begun clearing up the mess. Meanwhile, the 7.35am from Bristol in charge of Fairburn tank 42093 has been diverted onto the goods lines behind the station and Shipley passengers are using ladders to get off.

RIGHT: SUNDAY 4TH AUGUST, 1963, 12.7PM. Although it lost its regular passenger service in 1930, the Grassington branch continued to host excursion trains.

On a typically wet bank holiday weekend, Agecroft 'Crab' No. 42787 is almost slipping to a standstill while struggling unaided up the 1 in 90 out of Skipton station with the packed 10-coach 1X09 Manchester-Grassington.

The train is on the Skipton-Ilkley line and will take the Grassington branch at Embsay Junction, two miles ahead.

BELOW: 10TH AUGUST, 1963, 7.9PM. The CTAC excursions were a familiar sight in early 1960s West Riding. Here, the 1.57pm Gourock-Birmingham makes an unscheduled stop at Hellifield while Kingmoor Royal Scot 46160 *Queen Victoria's Rifleman* takes water. Kingmoor 'Black Five' 44986 stands in the Up platform with the 4.37pm Carlisle-Bradford slow.

The exclusive CTAC Scottish Tours Express trains ran to "Limited Load" timings and were accorded some priority towards punctual running. They were usually given at least class 6 power - sometimes class 8 because the civil engineer had recently authorised the use of A1 Pacifics on this route.

ABOVE: 24TH AUGUST, 1963, 6.41PM. Having worked the 10.34am Bournemouth-Bradford from Leicester Central, Jubilee 45708 *Resolution* recovers from a signal check and heads its train towards Huddersfield at Huddersfield Junction, Penistone.The electrified Woodhead line linking Sheffield and Manchester closed in 1981 and in 2003 only the Huddersfield line remained at this spot together with the shell of the signal box.

BELOW: 8TH NOVEMBER, 1963. A further stage in the gradual demise of the GN's Bradford-Keighley/Halifax via Queensbury lines which started with the withdrawal of regular passenger services and complete closure to normal traffic of the section between Cullingworth and Ingrow(just outside Keighley) in May, 1955.
Having shunted at Thornton with the 10.25am pick-up from Laisterdyke, WD 2-8-0 90721 leaves with the last loaded goods train to Cullingworth. The loco carries "The Economist" headboard, hand made by prize-winning Thornton stationmaster Bernard Whitaker in 1955 for the last passenger train to stop there. Before reaching its next port of call at Denholme, 90721 will climb to 877ft above sea level, the highest point on the whole GN. Goods traffic still ran between Bradford and Thornton until June, 1965. The last section of this fascinating system went in 1972 upon closure of the remaining stumps serving Great Horton and Bradford City Road.

ABOVE: 16TH NOVEMBER, 1963, 11.35AM. Not the image one normally associates with a football special - a bulled up Royal Scot heading a train which included a 12-wheel restaurant car - and for a game between two Fourth Division teams at that. The train is carrying Carlisle United supporters to a match at York City and Royal Scot 46118 *Royal Welch Fusilier* is pausing at Skipton's Up platform for water. The Scot was from Carlisle Upperby shed which was renowned for turning out spotless engines on football specials.

BELOW: 18TH APRIL, 1964 A spectacular view from above the eastern portals of Thackley Tunnel, between Apperley Bridge and Shipley. Holbeck Jubilee 45675 *Hardy* is deputising for yet another errant diesel, this time a BR Sulzer Type 2, while heading the 12.10pm St. Pancras-Bradford forward from Leeds. Apperley Viaduct signal box is in the middle distance with the branch to Esholt sewage works going off to the left.

ABOVE: 5TH MAY, 1964, 8.40AM. One of the two remaining BR Standard Class 5s in the Eastern and North Eastern regions - and the West Riding - 73163 of Huddersfield comes off the goods lines behind Shipley station and approaches Shipley Leeds Junction with the 8.10 Bradford Valley to Shipley Windhill class 9 freight. A local product, 73163 was built at Doncaster in 1957.

BELOW: 9TH MAY, 1964, 7.29AM. With just over 500 tons in tow, 'Black Five' 44694 blasts over Cutlers Junction, Laisterdyke, with the 7.19 Bradford-King's Cross excursion. The steam loco was booked to assist English Electric Type 4 D246 as far as Wakefield but the diesel had failed in the Laisterdyke area. As a result, 44694 was left having to single-handedly haul the train plus the dead 133-ton diesel and it's a safe bet the fireman was too busy to be looking out of his side of the cab!

ABOVE: 18TH MAY, 1964, 12.59PM. Kingmoor's rebuilt Patriot 45527 *Southport*, loaned to Blackpool shed for the occasion, bravely ascends the steep, sharply curved climb out of Skipton and up to Embsay with an 11-coach Preston-York excursion. The train had reached Skipton well before time and the booked assisting engine was still on shed. The Manningham men who had taken over at Colne got fed up with waiting and as they had the road, persuaded the guard to wave his flag and off they went - without the slightest trace of a slip.

BELOW: 29TH MAY, 1964, 1.56PM. After dieselisation of King's Cross services,the West Riding's remaining A1 Pacifics had very little work and were put in store. Some were returned to traffic in October, 1963 and kept quite busy covering diesel failures and special traffic. Nicely-groomed 60131 *Osprey*, now of Neville Hill, looks quite at home against the newly modernised Leeds City station as it departs with the 11am Liverpool-Newcastle via Harrogate. The train was steam-hauled because its diesel loco had derailed at Liverpool.

ABOVE: 2ND JUNE, 1964, 6.36PM. There is much speculation as to how many V2s reached Huddersfield on passenger trains but I think they could be counted on the fingers of one hand. One, No. 60929 arrives during a thunderstorm with the 1X46 Eastbourne-Leeds/Bradford which it had worked from Leicester Central. It was booked to work the Bradford portion but the route was prohibited to V2s so after much delay it took the Leeds portion. On reaching Leeds 60929 was declared unfit for service and sent light to its home depot at York.

BELOW: 12TH JUNE, 1964, 7.20PM. Southern Region Merchant Navy Pacific No. 35012 *United Sates Line* is surrounded by admirers at Holbeck shed after running light from London's Nine Elms depot - complete with Nine Elms men - to work the next day's Railway Correspendence & Travel Society "Solway Ranger" railtour. The engine's immaculate condition and sheer rarity earned it a round of applause.

ABOVE: 11TH JULY, 1964, 5.12PM. Class EM1 Bo-Bo electric locomotive 26037 speeds the 11.5am Yarmouth-Manchester express up through Deepcar on the 1500v dc electrified line from Sheffield to Manchester via Woodhead. When delivered new to the purpose-built depot at Wath-on-Dearne in 1952 for the newly electrified Woodhead line, these locomotives marked the start of modernisation in the West Riding and heralded the decline of the steam locomotive. Known affectionately as the 'Tommies' or 'Bo-Bos' their wheel arrangement was originally designated 0-4-4-0 and they remained in service until the Woodhead line closed in 1981.

BELOW: 12TH JULY, 1964, 5.16PM. Electrification and dieselisation on the West Coast main line had released the celebrated Coronation Pacifics from top link duties, making them available for railtours. No. 46255 *City of Hereford* makes an unusually fast pace through Calverley & Rodley with the Carlisle-Leeds leg of a Stephenson Locomotive Society special. These locomotives had always been extremely rare in the West Riding and this was the final visit of one under BR ownership as the last 17 examples were prematurely withdrawn less than three months later - despite several being in tip-top mechanical condition.

ABOVE: 25TH AUGUST, 1964. Grange 4-6-0 No. 6858 *Woolston Grange* rests on Huddersfield Hillhouse shed shortly before going light engine back to its native Western Region after making one of the most remarkable journeys ever recorded in the West Riding.

A strange set of circumstances meant that on 15th August 6858 ended up working the 8.55am Bournemouth-Leeds throughout from Oxford to Huddersfield. It should have been taken off the train at Nottingham Victoria but there was no replacement engine, and definitely at Sheffield Victoria - the absolute limit for WR locos owing to tight clearances on the line to Huddersfield. Still with no replacement it carried on, striking the platform at Denby Dale. Control ordered it removed at Huddersfield no matter what, for fear that it might hit the side of Morley Tunnel on the way to Leeds. No. 6858 was "hidden" on Hillhouse shed for 10 days while the authorities agonised over how to get it home. The full story is told in Railway Memories No.13.

BELOW: 6TH SEPTEMBER, 1964, 11.39AM. Lyons Maid "Zoom" ice lollies and loco spotting were an integral part of childhood at this time when cards depicting locos came free with the lollies and day trips ran for lolly consumers. Spotless Class 5 No. 44767, the only one with Stephenson link motion, drifts through the semaphore signals and on to the speed signalling zone at Heaton Lodge Junction, near Mirfield, with a Liverpool-York Lyons Maid Zoom special. The working notice carried the dire warning: "Special attention must be paid to the punctual running of this train" and it seems to have been heeded for it was running ahead of time.

ABOVE: 4TH OCTOBER, 1964, 16.39. Deputising for a prematurely withdrawn Coronation Pacific, Britannia No. 70020 *Mercury*, from London's Willesden shed, approaches Doncaster station in mercurial fashion on the Up Fast with the returning Home Counties Railway Societies special from York to King's Cross. It may have been the bowler-hatted loco inspector on the footplate or the York shedmaster who assured Control that engine and men were "up for it," but 70020 was given priority over the Deltic-hauled 13.56 Sunderland-King's Cross, hence the pace.

BELOW: 13TH OCTOBER, 1964, 14.10. An unusual combination at Huddersfield. Farnley Junction's Standard Class 3 2-6-0 No. 77012 and Stockport Jubilee 45655 *Keith* head a Crewe-bound 450-ton train of empty sleeper and restaurant cars returning off an overnight Plymouth-Darlington special. *Keith* was withdrawn six months later but 77012 survived to become one of the very last working steam locos at York shed in June, 1967.

ABOVE: 6TH MARCH, 1965, 11.05. A scene at Wakefield Kirkgate which would definitely not be tolerated nowadays. Jubilee 45698 *Mars* has uncoupled from the SLS/Manchester Locomotive Society Whitby Moors Rail Tour it has brought from Manchester as privately preserved LNER K4 2-6-0 No. 3442 *The Great Marquess* waits in the fish dock to take over.

Station master Fred Wilkinson - an absolute gentleman - came down from the platform and addressed the crowd: "Good morning gentlemen. Please take your photographs and return to the platform." In the meantime he had advised the signalmen to halt all trains as a safety precaution.

BELOW: 16TH MARCH, 1965, 12.05. Tragedy rather than diesel failure was the reason woebegone Jubilee 45666 *Cornwallis* of Warrington Dallam was on the 09.00 Liverpool-Newcastle, arriving at Huddersfield 96 minutes late. A railway clerk had been knocked down by the train at Kenyon Junction so a relief driver had to be found and the diesel loco detached at Patricroft for examination. No. 45666 was withdrawn the next month.

24th March, 1965: 'Peak' No. D167 on the 09.00 Liverpool-Newcastle failed completely in Huddersfield station. 'Black Five' 44695 took the train and its dead 'Peak' - 460 tons - forward to Leeds. Despite heavy rain and a 5mph p. way slack at Dewsbury, at the foot of the long climb to Morley Tunnel, it made Leeds in 35 minutes - just 5 minutes over the diesel timings and with the extra 138-ton dead weight of D167 - a remarkable achievement by the steam crew.

It was said that 44695 was being worked so hard from the Dewsbury slack that it could still be heard passing Lady Anne level crossing two miles away.

ABOVE: 17TH MARCH, 1965, 16.30. Three old engines preserved for the National Collection are moved from Derby Works to storage in the now closed Hellifield engine shed. Midland 4-2-2 No.118, London Tilbury & Southend 4-4-2T No. 80 *Thundersley* and Midland 2-4-0 No. 158A are seen being towed past Shipley Leeds Junction by BR Sulzer Type 2 No. D7597. The cavalcade was 223 minutes late due to frequent hot axlebox problems.

BELOW: 23RD APRIL, 1965, 19.02. A regular job for Patricroft Standard Class 5 4-6-0 No. 73006 was as Manchester Exchange station pilot but this included frequently being called to assist defective diesels over the Pennines to Huddersfield or Leeds, often twice in a day. In this case she was leaving Huddersfield in the dual role of assisting ailing EE Type 4 D256 with the 17.05 Liverpool-Newcastle and steam heating the train. Earlier that day, 73006 assisted 73158 on the 11.00 Liverpool-Newcastle following yet another diesel failure. The next day, she was back assisting 'Black Five' 44926 on the 11.00.

ABOVE: 29TH APRIL, 1965, 10.00. Neville Hill A1 Pacific 60131 *Osprey* was a rare visitor to Huddersfield. She is seen running round the empty coaches she brought tender first to form the 10.33 Huddersfield Choral Society special to King's Cross, which she worked as far as Doncaster.

BELOW: 7TH MAY, 1965, 18.27. By this time, the Fridays Only 17.38 Manchester -York had become a train to look out for as not only was it guarenteed steam but it was booked for a Carlisle Kingmoor engine. Seen leaving Huddersfield, it produced on this day one of the last two remaining rebuilt Patriot 4-6-0s, No. 45531 *Sir Frederick Harrison* which, like so many named steam locos now, was shorn of its nameplates.
No. 45531 was the last of the class to go through works, in April, 1963 after a decision to withdraw it had been reversed due to the poor availability of main line diesels. It was finally condemned in November, 1965.

ABOVE: 8TH MAY, 1965, 16.40. A further reward for keeping an eye on the 17.38 Fridays Only was that the loco could be seen returning to Manchester on the Saturday Newcastle-Red Bank empty vans. True to form, 45531 assists a Stanier Class 5 through Sowerby Bridge running the best part of 20 minutes early.

BELOW: 24TH JULY, 1965, 11.06. Having spent much of the winter in store A1 Pacific No. 60118 *Archibald Sturrock*, minus nameplates, passes Wortley Junction while in charge of the 09.30 Manchester-Newcastle via Harrogate. Ivatt Class 4 2-6-0 No. 43135 is waiting for the signal to leave the gas works sidings. This was the last summer for the West Riding A1s as all had been withdrawn by autumn.

ABOVE: 28TH AUGUST, 1965, 12.17. On the Settle & Carlisle and nearing the very northern limit of the old West Riding. Newton Heath 8F 2-8-0 No. 48557 battles with the wind as it hauls an engineers train past a solitary lengthman at wild and remote Blea Moor.

BELOW: 28TH AUGUST, 1965, 17.35. One of the last two surviving Royal Scots, No. 46115 *Scots Guardsman*, leaves Ribblehead Viaduct and climbs to Blea Moor with the 15.40 Bradford Forster Square-Carlisle slow conveying a Great Western 'Siphon' behind the engine. No. 46115 became the last Scot and was preserved, being delivered to the Keighley & Worth Valley Railway in August, 1966.

LEFT: 17TH SEPTEMBER, 1965, 17.38. The other remaining Royal Scot was 46140 *The King's Royal Rifle Corps*. This dramatic picture shows it during a violent thunderstorm while recovering from a signal check at Morley Low. It had been purloined to work the 1X48 Leeds to Blackpool illuminations special as far as Mirfield.

SHORT MEMORIES

30.9.63: Deputising for a failed Type 4 diesel, 'Black Five' 44982 of 10C Fleetwood brings the 3pm Liverpool-Newcastle into Leeds just 25 seconds late. The train is worked forward by A1 60154.

11.6.64: BR Caprotti 4-6-0 73136 of Derby reaches Wetherby with the pick-up goods.

RIGHT: 18TH SEPTEMBER, 1965. The N7 0-6-2Ts were designed for the intensive commuter service out of London Liverpool Street yet they were no strangers to the West Riding.

The final batch built at Doncaster in the late 1920s were run-in by Ardsley shed, and in 1954 Nos. 69691, 94, 95 and 96 were drafted to the Leeds area to cover for new diesel multiple units suffering teething troubles, working there on push-pull trains for about two years.

When 69621 was withdrawn in September, 1962 it was bought by Dr. Fred Youell for use on the Middleton Railway in Leeds, but it turned out to be too big and was stored in Neville Hill shed well into the 1970s.

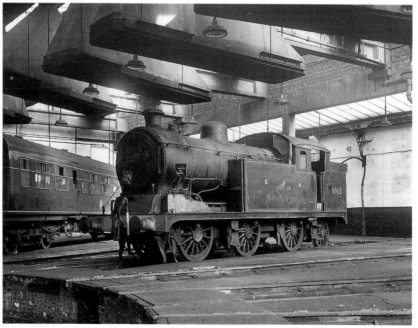

ABOVE: 21ST SEPTEMBER, 1965, 09.20. Game to the end - just days before being withdrawn, A1 No. 60154 *Bon Accord* was deputising for a failed Type 4 diesel when leaving Leeds City with the down North Briton to Glasgow. This was a train that all the big wigs from York headquarters travelled on to meetings in Darlington and Newcastle and it was considered unadvisable for them to be pulled by a dirty, rusty, broken-down old steam engine, so despite gaining time to York, 60154 was removed in favour of an English Electric Type 4 which failed at Durham. *Bon Accord* was withdrawn on 4th October after working only two more trains.

LEFT: 2ND NOVEMBER, 1965, 13.00. Passing Slaithwaite on the climb to Standedge Tunnel these three withdrawn locos are being dragged to their doom at Cashmore's of Great Bridge, Dudley, by 'Crab' 2-6-0 No. 42831.

The 4F, 43983 was booked to leave Royston shed at 09.00, Fowler 2-6-4T No. 42406 was collected at Wakefield, and sister loco 42317 at Huddersfield. Wakefield provided the towing engine and men plus two riders for the dead locos.

No. 42831 was herself withdrawn from service a month later and also broken up Cashmore's Great Bridge yard.

ABOVE: 2ND DECEMBER, 1965, 10.45. A wholly different procession of redundant engines. B1 4-6-0 No. 61386 was at Bradford Hammerton Street diesel depot manoeuvring Hunslet 0-6-0 shunters D2606, 04, 07, 03 and 05 in order to attach a brake van so they could be hauled up to Laisterdyke for reversal and onward transit to their new homes at Llanduno Junction and Holyhead.

BELOW: 11TH DECEMBER, 1965, 15.55. A dramatic vision of the gloom to come as the steam era descends into the darkness of oblivion. Long-time Royston engine, 8F No. 48222 passes its home depot and Royston & Notton signal box while pulling out of the yards with the 15.00 Carlton-Goole class 8 goods. Royston was to become one of the West Riding's last steam outposts.

ABOVE: 17TH MARCH, 1966, 1 1.59. By now the remaining steam locos were being run into the ground, receiving minimal maintenance. When one developed a fault it was usually withdrawn and a redundant loco sent from elsewhere to take its place. Fairburn tanks, for example, were drafted into the West Riding from other regions of BR. Here, 42074 - transferred from Chester - slogs up the 1 in 50 past Hammerton Street with the 11.55 Bradford-King's Cross. In the background is Adolphus Street goods yard and a fellow Fairburn tank descending towards the arched roof of the original passenger station with a short rake of vans.

This section of the bank includes a nasty curve believed to be briefly at 1 in 44 where on a bad rail anything could get bogged down. I've seen a B1 with just two coaches get stuck and I've seen and heard many a Deltic come to grief and require the assistance of a 204hp diesel shunter.

LEFT: 20TH APRIL, 1966, 12.55. DMU vehicles returning from Doncaster Works were conveyed in parcels trains to Bradford Exchange and then tripped up to Hammerton Street depot by any available loco. With 204hp diesel shunter D2152 on the right, Farnley Class 5 No.44826 propels Calder Valley driving motor E51819 onto the servicing road.

ABOVE: 21ST MAY, 1966, 08.40. The A4s had been vanquished from England but the remaining five were still on top link work in Scotland. In a return visit to the birthplace of this illustrious class, 60024 *Kingfisher*, chime whistle blowing, pulls out of platform 8 at Doncaster with an A4 Preservation Society special to Edinburgh.

BELOW: 2ND JULY, 1966, 16.35. As steam goes into rapid decline, summer Saturday expresses provide the final challenge for express passenger locomotives facing heavy loads on the steep and sinuous West Riding gradients. B1 No. 61115 assists Low Moor favourite, the ever-immaculate Jubilee 45565 *Victoria* and its 13.25 Bridlington-Bradford, up the bank from Greetland to Dryclough Junction, Halifax, which includes half a mile at 1 in 45.

ABOVE: 23RD JULY, 1966, 19.19. Jubilee No. 45562 *Alberta* passes Dodworth on the Barnsley-Penistone line with the celebrated 10.29 Poole-Bradford having successfully negotiated the 1 in 41 from Barnsley up to Summer Lane. On the left are connections to Dodworth Colliery where National Coal Board engines shunting out on to the main line ensured some form of steam working here well into the 1970s.

LEFT: 6TH AUGUST, 1966, 18.07. The southern edge of the West Riding and the Midland Railway's gateway to the county. Following a procession of diesel-hauled expresses, Jubilee 45562 *Alberta* emerges from Bradway Tunnel, clatters over Dore & Totley South Junction and makes for Sheffield when again heading the 10.29 Poole-Bradford which it was working from Nottingham.

The line in the foregound curves round to Totley Tunnel East Jn. and the Hope Valley route to Manchester.

ABOVE: 8TH OCTOBER, 1966, 14.05. The rare sight of a clean Wakefield WD. No. 90076 joins the Wakefield-Doncaster line at Hare Park Junction with the Locomotive Club of Great Britain Liverpool-Goole 'Crab Commemorative' railtour. The WD had taken over from 'Crab' 42942 at Wakefield Kirkgate.

BELOW: 8TH OCTOBER, 1966, 14.30. Wakefield was set to become one of the West Riding's last big steam sheds. Full of big steam shed atmosphere, this scene shows one of its Stanier 2-6-4Ts, No. 42664, alongside WD 90360 and an 8F 2-8-0 with B1 4-6-0s on each side.

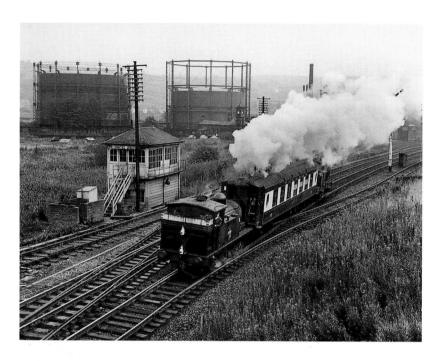

LEFT: 16TH OCTOBER, 1966, 11.45. Over the years, the North Eastern J72 0-6-0Ts have had a presence at several West Riding sheds, including Neville Hill, Selby, even Goole, Doncaster and Darnall as well as Normanton where they were used for trip working around Castleford. No. 69023, one of the batch built in 1950, was a former Newcastle station pilot and along with 69005 outlived the other J72s by going into departmental service. Here, as departmental No. 59 and having been named *JoEm* it passes Thwaites Junction, Keighley, on the final stage of its long journey from Heaton to preservation at the Worth Valley Railway. On the way it collected second class Pullman car No. 84 at York.

BELOW: 3RD DECEMBER, 1966, 11.15. Freights coming over the border from Lancashire would be the last BR steam trains in the West Riding. With a wintry foretaste of things to come, 8F 48707 has emerged from Kitson Wood Tunnel and is rolling down the 1 in 65 to Todmorden with the 10.15 White Birk-Healey Mills empties. This LMS-design engine was built in 1944 by the Southern Railway at Brighton for the LNER, becoming Class O6. Two years later it was handed over to the LMS but by 1952 had gone to BR's Western Region. After seven years it returned to the LM at Lostock Hall(Preston) where it ended its days.

RIGHT: 23RD JANUARY, 1967, 1 1.20-11.30.
Neville Hill P40 trip comprising 17 carflats loaded with 70 BMC vehicles from Longbridge for unloading in the car terminal at Garforth was stopped by signals when approaching from the Castleford branch. The guard applied his brake, destroying the vacuum which the engine, English Electric Type 3 No. D6792 was unable to fully recreate, leaving the train stuck across busy Garforth Junction with the loco's nose underneath the road bridge. In another tale of steam to the rescue, Normanton WD No. 90615 was sent with a brake van from its trip duty at Neville Hill. The car train was divided, the diesel working forward with the front portion and the WD propelling the rear portion.

BELOW: 27TH MARCH, 1967, 14.12. It came as a pleasant surprise that several of the Anglo-Scottish Easter reliefs were booked for steam north of Leeds. In the event, some were diesel hauled but Easter Monday's 09.20 St. Pancras-Glasgow relief was entrusted to Kingmoor Britannia Pacific 70053 *Moray Firth*. It appeares to have been suffering from dubious coal when passing Kirkstall power station and Armley(Canal Road) No.2 signal box.

ABOVE: 15TH APRIL, 1967, 10.27. Viewed from the footplate of Fairburn tank 42152 leaving Leeds with the final leg of the 06.40 Birmingham-Bradford, is Stanier Class 5 No. 45296 from Wigan Springs Branch on the Bradford-Leeds leg of the up Devonian. Its worried-looking fireman no doubt isn't used to someone pointing a camera at him from the cab of an oncoming locomotive and will be hoping I withdraw my head in time. On the right are Gelderd signal box and the remains of Holbeck Low Level station which closed in 1958.

BELOW: 27TH APRIL, 1967, 10.30. Against a classic West Riding backdrop of mill chimneys, Ivatt Class 4 2-6-0 No. 43117 climbs away from Shipley Windhill with the daily trip to Idle. This was the last week of steam on the Idle branch which closed completely on 5th October, 1968. The Leeds-Skipton line is down on the right.

ABOVE: 28TH APRIL, 1967, 13.25. Passed fireman Ivan Maltby uses Manningham shed's primitive coal stage to fill the bunker of Fairburn 2-6-4T No. 42138. This was one of the last times the old coaler would be used for the depot closed the next day.

BELOW: 28TH APRIL, 1967, 18.39. From the start of the 1966 winter timetable the 18.25 from Leeds (13.50 St. Pancras-Bradford Forster Square) was one of the last dozen or so steam passenger diagrams in the North Eastern Region and I enjoyed plenty of footplating on it. On the last day it ran through to Bradford, it was hauled by one of Manningham's Fairburn 2-6-4Ts and 42152 is seen storming across Whitehall Junction just after leaving Leeds City. The maroon coaching stock livery is rapidly giving way to the new blue and white.

ABOVE: SATURDAY 29TH APRIL, 1967, 16.27. This was the day when a lot of fires went out in the West Riding for it was the end of main line services to Bradford Forster Square, the closure of Manningham shed and from the following Monday the dieselisation of all local trip workings. Here, Kingmoor Britannia Pacific 70031 *Byron* with homemade numberplates and painted "nameplates" prepares to work the last steam-hauled main line passenger train out of Forster Square, the 16.30 to Birmingham.

BELOW: 23RD MAY, 1967, 10.53. Many changes have taken place. Leeds Central closed on 1st May and all passenger trains now use City station, the Bradford portions of King's Cross trains also run to and from Leeds City instead of Wakefield and the 07.45 through train from King's Cross is diagrammed for steam-diesel double heading over the arduous Leeds-Bradford Exchange line. Here the train has just left Leeds City and Fairburn 2-6-4T No. 42066 is vigorously assisting BR Sulzer Type 2 No. D5100 on the climb up past Holbeck Junction and (on the left) the disused remains of the line into Central.

ABOVE 29TH MAY, 1967, 08.46. The approaching summer promises one last chance for steam-hauled express passenger trains. This splendidly panoramic view shows Stanier Class 5 4-6-0 No. 44693 battling up the 1 in 50 away from Bradford Exchange with the 1X08 excursion to Blackpool. In the foreground are St. Dunstan's signal box, the carriage sidings and the remains of St. Dunstan's station, and beyond the train are Mill Lane box and Spring Mill Street goods yard.

BELOW: 29TH MAY, 1967, 09.50. Despite the large numbers allocated to the area, double headed 2-6-4Ts were fairly rare. Nos. 42066 and 42073 are double heading 1Z58, the 09.43 Bradford Exchange-Bridlington excursion up the bank to Laisterdyke simply because Low Moor had run out of serviceable tender engines.

ABOVE: 29TH JULY, 1967, 08.22. With steam having ended on the Southern Region's main line out of Waterloo, the West Riding, in particular the Bradford area, had become the most densely populated steam passenger area in the country and was becoming a popular haunt for enthusiasts. With sights like this, who could blame them! A five shilling bribe persuading the driver of the lighter-loaded 'Black Five' 44662 to hold back ensured the awesome spectacle of two 08.20 departures from Bradford Exchange storming up to Mill Lane neck and neck. The Skegness train with 44662 is on the right and sister 44694 with the Bridlington train is on the left. Between them, Sulzer Type 2 No. D5251 has empty stock for the 09.00 to King's Cross.

BELOW: 5TH AUGUST, 1967, 09.09. By now Low Moor had the last three operational B1s in existance(departmental locos apart) but it had no passenger diagrams for them. By kind arrangement, 61306 was turned out for the 09.06 Bradford-Poole as far as Huddersfield and for the benefit of tape recorders made a rousing ascent of the 1 in 50 to Bowling Junction, as seen here. The following month 61306 was withdrawn and spent several months stored at Normanton before going to Carnforth for preservation.

ABOVE: 19TH AUGUST, 1967, 14.40. The persuasive nature of the traction engineer at Leeds, the likeable Tom Greaves, was almost certainly the reason why three summer Saturday reliefs over the Settle & Carlisle were diagrammed to Holbeck Jubilees. Things didn't always go per diagram because the odd Britannia popped up or a spare diesel but there was a fair chance of two being Jubilee-hauled. By now they were the only trains in the country to be hauled by express passenger steam locos. No. 45593 *Kolhapur* roars through Keighley with one of those trains, the 09.20 St. Pancras-Glasgow.

BELOW: 21ST AUGUST, 1967, 12.20. Clearance tests were being run with Great Western-design 4-6-0 No. 7029 *Clun Castle* with a view to it being used on a programme of railtours in the area. With name and number plates removed, the privately-preserved loco is seen propelling the gauging saloon - a converted horsebox - past Shipley Leeds Junction while en-route to Steeton & Silsden, making it the first ever visit of a Western Region engine to this line.

SHORT MEMORIES

12.67: The 01.40 Carlisle- Stourton and 13.10 Carlisle-Skipton freights are regular Kingmoor Britannia turns.

31.12.67: Normanton shed is closed to steam. Visiting London Midland Region locomotives despatched immediately back to the Manchester area are three dead Class 5s and a 9F 2-10-0 hauled by Class 5 No. 44834, and a dead Class 5 plus two 9Fs hauled by No. 44889.

ABOVE: 2ND SEPTEMBER, 1967, 16.16. Steam-hauled for the very last time, the 13.25 Bridlington-Bradford is brought out of Dryclough Tunnel and up the 1 in 45 from Greetland by 'Black Five' 44662 which was taking things easy and letting the banking engine, an English Electric Type 3 diesel, do most of the work. Throughout the summer, crews, realising that history was being made, entered into the spirit of things. This train, for example, arrived at Greetland 20 minutes early to await the banker.

BELOW: 21ST SEPTEMBER, 1967, 15.40. Royston motive power depot and neighbouring Carlton and Cudworth yards had become one of the last bastions of steam in Britain. On the former Hull & Barnsley Railway, an 8F 2-8-0 is propelling a heavy load of coal into Cudworth yard, past Cudworth Yard South Junction signal box.

ABOVE: 9TH OCTOBER, 1967, 11.15. A familiar 1960s scene. We all remember the last months of steam but how many remember the brake tenders which many diesels needed to improve their braking power with heavy loose-coupled freights? English Electric Type 3 No. D6949 stands with brake tenders at Healey Mills yard as Newton Heath 8F 2-8-0 No. 48321 awaits departure on the 11.10 coal to Middleton Junction, near Manchester. Very soon, most West Riding steam workings would be freights between Lancashire and Healey Mills.

BELOW: 4TH NOVEMBER, 1967, 11.30. After this day, the London Midland Region was the only one on BR still operating steam locomotives but they would continue to reach the West Riding to the very end of BR steam in August, 1968. The Eastern Region retained limited servicing facilities at Normanton for visiting steam locomotives until the end of 1967. One such visitor, Birkenhead 9F 2-10-0 No. 92094, has its tender filled among the diesels as enginemen discuss the rapidly changing scene.

At the end of 1967, the West Riding's last passenger trains booked for steam went over to diesels - the 03.32MX Leeds-Halifax & 04.38MX Halifax-Manchester Victoria, the 17.47FO Manchester Victoria-York and the 23.38 Sun. Liverpool-Leeds. It was reported that from 4th March, 1968 the 03.32MX Leeds-Halifax and 04.38MX Halifax-Manchester Vic. were booked for a Newton Heath Class 5, possibly returning off a freight to Healey Mills. They were reported to finally be diesel from 20th May.

ABOVE: 4TH NOVEMBER, 1967. The last steam locomotive to be operated in traffic by the Eastern Region, 8F 2-8-0 No.48276, makes a ghostly return to its home depot at Royston and inevitable withdrawal after working the region's last steam train, the 15.00 Carlton to Goole freight.

While 4th November, 1967 is generally accepted as the end of Eastern Region steam, B1 4-6-0s Nos. 61050(now No.30) and 61315(now No. 32) were still in departmental service, being used for carriage heating at Sheffield's Nunnery sidings.
Nominally allocated to Canklow depot, they got water at Rotherham Masborough but had to go to Normanton for coal. Their speed during these main line movements was severely restricted.
When not in use they were stabled in a siding between Masborough station and Holmes Junction.
No.30 was last used in mid-December, 1967 when it joined the Normanton scrap line. No.32 last saw use on 8th January, 1968 making it technically the last steam locomotive used by the Eastern Region.

LEFT: 4TH NOVEMBER, 1967. The Eastern Region's last steam men say farewell to 48276 inside Royston shed after their final trip to Goole and back.
From left, they are: driver Geoff Ellis, guard Denniss Duncan and fireman Gerald Harris. At ground level, shedmaster Ted Camp joins the far from sad group.

LEFT: SATURDAY 23RD DECEMBER, 1967. The London Midland Region surprised everybody and delighted many by diagramming steam for several trans-Pennine Christmas relief trains.

In this quite remarkable scene, Patricroft Class 5 No. 45073 drops down to Holbeck Junction with the 1N76 09.30 Manchester-Newcastle relief as Newton Heath's 45055 comes storming up the bank out of Leeds with the 1M52 09.20 Darlington-Manchester relief. There couldn't have been many occasions by this time when two steam-hauled express passenger trains would pass each other.

BELOW: 16TH MARCH, 1968, 18.05. The year dawned with about 10 steam freights reaching Healey Mills yard each day but only two to Leeds. As Normanton shed had closed completely, visiting LMR engines were turned, watered and sent back as soon as possible. Carnforth 9F No. 92077 had worked in with the 12.12 Heysham-Hunslet oil tanks and was being photographed while passing Leeds City on its way home with the empties.

ABOVE: 28TH JULY, 1968, 14.42. Every Saturday from March to August had at least one steam special booked and some days there were three. One of the last was this Manchester Rail Travel Societies special seen being hurried up the bank southbound from Hellifield by Standard Class 4 4-6-0s 75019 and 75027. The pair had been regulars on the Grassington branch until steam finished there in June and on 31st May 75019 worked the last BR steam freight over the Settle & Carlisle - a ballast train from Swinden quarry to Appleby.

BELOW: 28TH JULY, 1968, 18.49. Later in the day, the above special was taken from Rose Grove back to Manchester by much-travelled 8F No. 48773, seen here pulling briskly away from Todmorden.
Built in 1940 for the Ministry of Supply by the North British Locomotive Company in Glasgow, it saw considerable action in the Middle East during the second world war and did not return home until 1952. After a further five years on the Longmoor Military Railway, Hants, it was sold to BR.

LEFT: 11TH AUGUST, 1968, 12.57. The end. The very last standard gauge train hauled by a British Rail steam locomotive, the never-to-be-forgotten "15 Guinea Special" heads towards Blea Moor Tunnel with Britannia Pacific 70013 *Oliver Cromwell* in charge.

BELOW: 25TH FEBRUARY, 1969. K1 62005 and K4 3442 *The Great Marquess* were waiting at Holbeck depot to enter the Hunslet Engine Co.'s works where the K1 was to donate its boiler to the K4. It was found not to be necessary and both engines still survive in preservation.

Never allocated to Holbeck, 62005 first appeared there on 17th August, 1967 but was back in the North East for railtours on 9th September, the day steam finished there. It returned to Holbeck the next day still wearing a 52H Tyne Dock shedplate but on 13th September was seen passing Eaglescliffe light engine. Returning to Holbeck on the 17th, it was still there in company with six other steam locos on 4th November, by which time Holbeck was officially closed to steam. Boxing Day saw it hired to Phillips oil refinery at North Tees as a stationary boiler. It was not officially withdrawn until December, 1967, making it another candidate for the last Eastern Region steam loco!

No. 3442 was stored at Neville Hill but later in 1968 both locos were inside Holbeck shed. They were moved outdoors ready for the roundhouses to be demolished in February and March, 1969.

ABOVE: 1ST JUNE, 1969, 10.36. After 11th August, 1968, the A3 *Flying Scotsman* was the only steam loco permitted by BR to run on its standard gauge network. This was because when withdrawn in 1963 it was bought by Alan Pegler who secured an agreement from the BR Board allowing it to run on the main lines until 1971. As most lineside locomotive watering facilities had been removed by this time, it was equipped with a second tender for carrying an extra supply.

With main line steam finished *Flying Scotsman* was much in demand. It is seen at Dryclough Junction, Halifax, heading an ambitious Doncaster-Halifax-Manchester-Carlisle-Newcastle-Leeds-Doncaster railtour which included a stop for coal at Haltwhistle on the Carlisle-Newcastle line.

Looking back, we can now see this was the start of a whole new era for main line steam.

LEFT: 29TH JUNE, 1969, 15.30. During a special run to celebrate the first year of public services on the Keighley & Worth Valley Railway, *Flying Scotsman* draws its empty train out of the Worth Valley platforms at Keighley prior to setting back into the main line part of station. Less than three months later it set sail from Liverpool for its tour of the USA.